T0108880

The Writings of Frithjof Schuon
Series

World Wisdom
The Library of Perennial Philosophy

The Library of Perennial Philosophy is dedicated to the exposition of the timeless Truth underlying the diverse religions. This Truth, often referred to as the *Sophia Perennis*—or Perennial Wisdom—finds its expression in the revealed Scriptures as well as the writings of the great sages and the artistic creations of the traditional worlds.

Autumn Leaves & The Ring appears in our series entitled The Writings of Frithjof Schuon.

The Writings of Frithjof Schuon

The Writings of Frithjof Schuon series form the foundation of our library because he is the pre-eminent exponent of the Perennial Philosophy. His work illuminates this perspective in both an essential and comprehensive manner like none other.

Autumn Leaves
&
The Ring

Poems by
Frithjof Schuon

German-English Edition

Introduction by
Patrick Laude

Autumn Leaves and The Ring
Poems by Frithjof Schuon
©2010 World Wisdom, Inc.

All rights reserved.
No part of this book may be used or reproduced
in any manner without written permission,
except in critical articles and reviews.

Library of Congress Cataloging-in-Publication Data

Schuon, Frithjof, 1907-1998.
[Poems. English & German. Selections]
Autumn leaves & the ring : poems / by Frithjof Schuon ; introduction by Patrick Laude. -- German-English ed.
p. cm. -- (The writings of Frithjof Schuon) (The library of perennial philosophy)
Includes index.
ISBN 978-1-935493-17-4 (pbk. : alk. paper) 1. Schuon, Frithjof, 1907-1998--Translations into English. I. Title. II. Title: Autumn leaves and the ring.
PT2680.U474A2 2010
831'.914--dc22
2010008339

Cover art: Detail from a painting by Frithjof Schuon

Printed on acid-free paper in USA

For information address World Wisdom, Inc.
P.O. Box 2682, Bloomington, Indiana 47402-2682

www.worldwisdom.com

Contents

Frithjof Schuon

Introduction

The German poems of Frithjof Schuon constitute a metaphysical and spiritual summa which brings together the essential teachings of this master in a form that is at once accessible and direct. This poetry is accessible not as a facile and ultimately fruitless work of vulgarization would be, but rather because it aims at the simplicity of the essence; such synthetic simplicity lies beyond the conceptual and formal complexity of Schuon's prose works, for his essays weave together multiple dimensions and ramifications, taking account of a diversity of aspects and points of view. Indeed, complexity, like simplicity, has its role to play in the economy of spiritual means, and Schuon had little affinity with hasty or overly pedagogical simplifications. Nevertheless, the quintessential esoterism that he presents to us is "simple" with the bare simplicity of truth. Schuon's poetry espouses this simplicity and provides us with a musical distillation of the elixir of wisdom, while his prose works feed us with a dense, rich and diverse substance. These are, as it were, the liquid and solid "species" of his teachings: his wine and bread. His poetry is direct, not in that it would bypass a discernment between levels of reality and the need for spiritual mediations, but inasmuch as it gives precedence to aesthetic vibrations and "mental beauty," to use Schuon's characterization of poetry. It does this by joining essence to form, by "musicalizing" the conceptual geometry of the doctrine in order to lodge it at the deepest core of the soul, without detours and dialectical precautions. In its directness and simplicity, poetry may appear to us as an ultimate mercy, a last saving rope held out to us. It is the mercy of a sage whose life and work can only be understood as a gift, a gift often sacrificial and all too frequently not understood. It transmits a nucleus of certitudes which provide the key to happiness in this world and the next.

It must be acknowledged that Schuon's German poetry cannot be translated into other languages—and especially Romance languages, whose genius is so different from that of Germanic languages—without being deprived of a large part of its aesthetic power of interiorization. However, the synthetic simplicity of what is transmitted retains its didactic power in translation, since the form must remain in the last analysis subordinate to the content, as in all traditional poetry. As far as translation is concerned, Schuon himself has enunciated guiding principles in one of his later works. In the chapter "On the Art of Translating" in *To Have a Center* he indicates that translating poetry does not mean producing a fusion of form and content that would be analogous to that of the original, but merely transmitting the content as faithfully as possible.

According to Schuon, poetry can de defined as an art in which the essence "moves" in the direction of the form, in the sense that the perception of an archetype is crystallized in the images, and even in the rhythm of the poem: "In poetry the musicality of realities, or their cosmic essentiality, erupts on the plane of language." By contrast with poetry, in music and dance it is the form which "moves" in the direction of the essence: the melodic, rhythmic and harmonic unfolding points to the essence, whether through emotional fusion, through the reduction of multiplicity to unity, or else by conformation to the very structure of our deepest being. As Schuon writes in one of his poems, music is successively joy in multiplicity and nostalgia for the One, and these two aspects converge in our inebriation with the Infinite. By virtue of this principle of extinctive and unitive inebriation, Schuon can define music as the flow of accidents back to the Substance. On the plane of subjective perception, this flowing-back is to be understood as a remembrance of our most profound nature.

In poetry, by contrast, the infusion of the essence into the form accounts for the fact that there is no traditional poetics which does not subordinate the container to the content, be this content envisaged as "harmony" (*sāman*) in India, "natural principle" (*li*) in China, or "inner meaning" (*maʿnā*) in Islam. In all great poetry the essence determines the linguistic form over which it takes precedence, while integrating the form to the inner perception of the poet.

In distinction to sacred scriptures, in which—in Schuon's terms—human language "bursts" under the pressure of divine inspiration, poetry structures and incorporates language to its own intent. In order for this to happen, the poet must nevertheless experience an inner pressure. During the last years of his life, Schuon produced a major poetic work in his native language—German—while expressing in several instances his wish to see it come to a close. The inspiration had an aspect of necessity that seemed to impose itself upon the poet's will. It is not unusual to see spiritual masters exteriorize thus their message *in fine*, in a synthetic and direct manner which casts into relief the spiritual urgency of the ever present proximity of death—a proximity ever eluded by fallen man.

This is a kind of essential recapitulation that finds in the poetic genre a form perfectly adapted to its end. It is moreover mainly in brief forms that such a coincidence between essential content and synthetic form is actualized. The most beautiful poetry is a "gem of perfection and a vibration of infinity." In it, as in every form of beauty, an encounter between absoluteness and infinity takes place. In the West, it is often in the sonnet—with such as Dante and Shakespeare—that a maximum of formal contraction is combined with the vastest fullness of meaning. Schuon's poetry also is characterized by its vigorous and suggestive concision. In this respect, it is possible to compare Schuon's mode of expression with those of Angelus Silesius and Lalla Yogishvari.

Lalla's *vakhs* are short pieces of four verses, while the *Cherubinischer Wandersmann*, composed by the seventeenth-century German mystic and even more informed by intuitive concision, is composed in distichs. We find thus in Schuon something of a poetic convergence between the German mysticism of the Essence—the most imaginatively bold Christianity, and the most jnanic, in a sense—and the mystical femininity of India: two fundamental poles of the spiritual archetype expressed by his artistic personality.

In Lalla as in Silesius, poetic expression is characterized not only by a certain formal concision, but also by clarity and sobriety, together with an incisive vigor of images. There is to be found, too, an audacious and implacable quality in the modes of spiritual expression. Accordingly, Frithjof Schuon's poetry is less allusive—as Zen-like Japanese poetry can be, particularly the *haiku*—than didactic and symbolic. It therefore emphasizes the continuity between the spiritual intuition and its linguistic expression, rather than seeking to disarticulate or "burn" the latter toward "apophatic" ends. This aspect of Schuon's poetry is no doubt related to the normative and integrative function that devolves upon the *logos* and intelligence in Schuon's spiritual perspective. Similarly, the intellective concision of his poetic work accounts for the fact that Schuon does not demonstrate major affinities with the exuberance of images and wealth of symbols of most Sufi poetry, notwithstanding the fact that he wrote some mystical poetry in Arabic as well. For him, it is rather a matter of producing a poetry in which form is solidly informed by content.

Schuon does recognize the polysemic mystery of poetry as such—this is evidenced by his choice of Dante's verses "*mirate la dottina che s'asconde/ sotto 'l velame de li versi strani* ("Consider the doctrine that is hidden/ Under the veil of strange verses") as an epigraph. However, he does not place as much of an emphasis upon it as do the majority of contemporary poets, most likely because he wants to parry the fashionable literary relativism that is so pervasive in modern culture. Be that as it may, the fact that the greater part of Schuon's poetry was composed in his native German suggests the extent to which poetry is for him the language of the soul, both individually and collectively. By contrast his essays, almost entirely written in French, pertain to the intellect, or at any rate to reason inasmuch as it reflects the intellect. The respective virtues that Schuon attributes to German and French refer on the one hand to a power of symbolic and imaginative evocation—which ultimately relates to the psycho-spiritual—and on the other hand to analytic precision—which is consonant with the conceptual expression of spiritual realities.

Schuon's early poetry—mainly that of his collection *Sulamith*—was spiritually indebted to the *Song of Songs*, while also echoing German Romanticism and *Sturm und Drang*; it was perhaps more centered upon the aspect "perception" than upon the aspect "transmission," at least in the sense that it was more obviously akin to a "drunkenness" with archetypes than a concern for teaching. The poetry of his later years, his sapiential and poetic testament, is more didactic and characterized by sobriety, and thereby more easily and universally accessible. It is most likely so because it is less "subjective" and more focused on the pole "mode of assimilation" than on the pole "mode of perception." Thus, it highlights a type of synthetic teaching that is complementary in relation to what is dispensed in his essays. The frequent use of the second person—to be found in Angelus Silesius and to a lesser extent in Lalla Yogishvari—bears witness to the didactic nature of this poetry, while at the same time conveying a perfume of spiritual testament and personal presence, or even spiritual intimacy; more profoundly still, it manifests an intellective perspective in which the soul is as it were "objectified" as an interlocutor by the Intellect or the Spirit.

—Patrick Laude

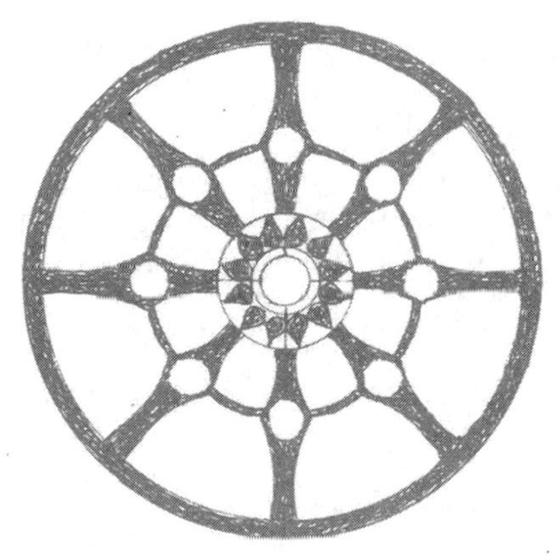

Wiederholt

Was ich hier sagen möcht — mit euch der Friede! —
Das findet sich in einem frühern Liede:

Frühling und Herbst: Pole in Daseins Raum —
Ins Alter hat das Schicksal mich gelenkt.
Müde und selbstlos ist des Lebens Baum —
Herbstblätter sind wie Gold, das sich verschenkt.

Seid nicht betrübt, wenn Lebens Sommer scheidet —
O Friede, der die Seel mit Gold bekleidet!

Manuscript page in the author's hand

Herbstblätter

Autumn Leaves

I

Schönheit

Beauty

Wiederholt

Was ich hier sagen möcht — mit euch der Friede! —
Das findet sich in einem frühern Liede:

Frühling und Herbst: Pole in Daseins Raum —
Ins Alter hat das Schicksal mich gelenkt.
Müde und selbstlos ist des Lebens Baum —
Herbstblätter sind wie Gold, das sich verschenkt.

Seid nicht betrübt, wenn Lebens Sommer scheidet —
O Friede, der die Seel mit Gold bekleidet!

Vita Nuova

Nicht immer ist der Liebe Sinn Besitz;
Du kannst Geliebtes auch im Herzen tragen,
Wie Dante Beatrix, ein Leben lang;
Der Liebe Pulse können einsam schlagen.

Wohl muss die Seel auf Erden mit sich ringen —
Irdisches muss dem Himmel näher bringen.
Die Herzenstiefe ist das Elixier —

„Gibt es ein Paradies auf Erden, ist es hier."

Repeated

What I would like to say here – may Peace be with you! –
Is also found in an earlier song:

Spring and autumn: poles in the space of existence –
Destiny has led me into old age.
Weary and selfless is the tree of life –
Autumn leaves are like gold that gives itself away.

Do not be saddened when life's summer departs –
O Peace, that clothes the soul in gold!

Vita Nuova

The meaning of love is not always possession;
Thou canst carry the belovèd also in thy heart,
As Dante did Beatrice, a whole life long;
The pulse of love can beat in solitude.

Truly the soul must struggle with itself on earth –
Earthly things must bring us nearer Heaven.
The depth of the heart is the elixir –

"If there is a Paradise on earth, it is here."

Der Fächer

Das Öffnen eines Fächers sagt, dass sich
Die Welt entfaltet, Schöpfungswunder zeigend:
Oder wie sich die Göttin offenbart,
Amaterasu, aus dem Meere steigend –

So wie in uns der Geist, der sich entfaltet,
Sein Licht in goldnen Bildern neu gestaltet.
Der Fächer schließt sich, wie ein Sang verklingt;
So wie die Sonne spät im Meer versinkt.

So mag der Geist, nach der Entfaltung Scheinen,
Selig zurückkehrn zu dem Großen Einen.

Fiat

Ist es nicht seltsam, dass wir insgeheim
Etwas in unsrem Erdenleiden lieben?
Ein Etwas ist vom ersten Sündenfall,
Von seiner Not, in unsrem Herz geblieben.

Wir fühlen Schönheit in Melancholie –
In unsrer Kunst, in unsren Sehnsuchtsliedern.
Es ist, als wollten wir des Leidens Muss
Mit unsrer Seele tiefem Ja erwidern.

The Fan

The opening of a fan tells how the world
Unfolds to show the marvels of creation;
Or how the goddess manifests herself,
Amaterasu, rising from the sea –

Just as in us the Spirit, self-unfolding,
Shapes its light anew in golden pictures.
The fan closes upon itself, like a song fading away,
Like the sun sinking late into the sea.

So may the Spirit, after its unfolding,
Blissfully return to the Great One.

Fiat

Is it not strange how we secretly
Love something in our earthly suffering?
A something from man's first fall,
And its misery, has remained in our heart.

We feel beauty in melancholy –
In our art and in our nostalgic songs;
It is as if we wished to answer the "must" of suffering
With the deep "yes" of our soul.

Körperseele

Des Menschen Körper: Glorie, Niedrigkeit,
Verbinden sich. Zuerst, was Gott gewollt;
Und dann, was Erdendasein mit sich bringt –
Bedenkt, was ihr als Mensch verkörpern sollt!

Versteht, dass nur des Schöpfers Absicht gilt –
Dann habt ihr eures Daseins Sinn erfüllt.
Körper der Seele: das, was äußerlich;
Seele des Körpers: das gesamte Ich.

Urbilder

Geliebte Menschen stehen in den Sternen
Geschrieben, in den tiefen Raum gemalt;
Sie waren schon, bevor sie irdisch waren –
Die Namen Gottes sind ihr Urgehalt.

Sie liebend, liebst du Gott, ob du es weißt
Oder nicht weißt. Gott liebend, liebst du sie –
Denn sie sind Bilder, die der Höchste schuf
Aus seinem Wesensgrund – du weißt nicht wie

Man es soll nennen. Gott ist unermesslich:
Der Eine ist Unendlichkeit – so höre
Das Rätsel – Er ist unergründlich reich,
Ohne dass sich das Eine Sein vermehre.

Body-Soul

The human body: glory and low estate
Combine. First what God willed,
And then what earthly existence brings with it —
Think, what as human beings you should embody!

Understand that only the Creator's intention counts —
Then you have fulfilled the meaning of your existence.
Body of the soul: what is outward;
Soul of the body: the complete I.

Archetypes

Belovèd human beings are written in the stars,
Painted in deep space;
They were already, before they were earthly —
The Divine Names are their quintessence.

In loving them, thou lovest God, whether thou knowest it
Or not. In loving God, thou lovest them —
For they are images created by the Most High
Out of His Nature's depth — thou knowest not how

To describe this. God is unfathomable:
The One is Infinite — so listen
To the riddle — He is inexhaustibly rich,
Without the One multiplying Itself.

Parabel

Es kam ein Barde, der von Liebe sang;
Er blieb an meines Hauses Türe stehen.
Er sang ein Lied, das mir ins Herze drang –
Die Winde hörten auf zu wehen.

So ist es, wenn die Liebe Gottes kommt
Und unsrer Seele Türe öffnen will,
Mit einer Gnade, die dem Herzen frommt –
Des Welttrugs Winde stehen still.

Anziehung

Was ist es, was der Mann im Weibe liebt?
Es ist das Andere – es ist das Gleiche.
Er liebt die Kindlichkeit und das Geheimnis;
Doch auch was gilt im männlichen Bereiche –
Den Geist, die Kraft; den Willen, die Erkenntnis
Im Kleid der Schönheit.
Liebe zieht mich hin
Zum Anderen – zu dem auch, was ich bin.

Gleichnis

So wie die Schöne bei der Liebe Fest
Die Seide von den Schultern gleiten lässt –
Die Nacht ist Kleid, die Sonne ist die Blöße.
Der Leib: als Gottes Ebenbild gewoben –
Das Urbild ist beim Höchsten aufgehoben.

Im reinen Sein erstrahlt der Gottheit Größe.

Parable

There came a minstrel who sang of love;
He stood before the door of my house.
He sang a song that pierced my heart –
The winds all ceased to blow.

So it is when God's Love appears,
And seeks to open the door of our soul
With a grace that heals our heart –
The winds of the world-illusion stand still.

Attraction

What is it that man loves in woman?
What is different – and what is the same.
He loves childlikeness and mystery,
But also what counts in the masculine domain –
Mind, strength; will, knowledge
In the garment of beauty.
Love draws me
Towards the other – but also to what I am.

Likeness

Just as the fair one at the feast of love
Lets the silk slip from her shoulders –
So is the night a garment, and the sun an unveiling.
The body is woven as the image of God –
The archetype is in the keeping of the Most High.

In pure Being shines forth the Godhead's greatness.

Schönheiten

Ein nacktes Weib und geigende Zigeuner –
Ein schönes Bild, davon man träumen kann.
Noch andre Schönheit bietet uns die Erde –
Ein Psalm mit Harfe und ein heilger Mann.

Die Welt ist vielgestaltig, wunderlich –
Das Heilige ist eine Welt für sich.

Rādhākrishna

Rādhā im heilgen Hain. Und Krishna kam;
Sein Antlitz strahlte wie die Morgenröte.
Er spielt ein Lied auf seiner Zauberflöte –
Ein Sehnsuchtslied, das ihr die Sinne nahm.

Sie wurden eins im heilgen Liebestrieb –
Die Welt erlosch. Nur noch Ānanda blieb.

Kuan-Yin

Erst ungeschlechtlich, dann als Weib verstanden,
Wird Avalokitèshwara verehret
Im Mahāyāna – eine Kundgebung
Der Güte, die von uns das Böse wehret.

Kuan-Yin: auf einem Himmelslotos sitzend,
Versunken tief in ihre eigne Mitte;
Es strahlen ihre gnadenvollen Brüste,
Ihr goldner Leib, die Heiligen beschützend.

Ihr gleicht die Tārā – andre Lotosblüte
Des Ostens, Strahlenkranz der lichten Güte;
Barmherzigkeit in wechselnden Gestalten –
Doch überall.
Lass deine Gnade walten.

Beauties

A naked woman and gypsy violins –
A beautiful image of which one can dream.
Yet other beauties the earth offers us –
A psalm with a harp, and a holy man.

The world is multiform, and wondrous –
The sacred is a world unto itself.

Rādhākrishna

Rādhā in the sacred grove. And Krishna came;
His face was shining like the blush of dawn.
He played a song upon his magic flute –
A longing song, that robbed her of her senses.

They became one in their sacred play of love –
The world was extinguished. Only *Ānanda* remained.

Kwan-Yin

First without gender, then perceived as woman,
Thus Avalokitèshwara is venerated
In the *Mahāyāna* – a manifestation
Of Goodness that averts from us the bad.

Kwan-Yin: seated on a heavenly lotus,
Sunk deep in her own center;
Her merciful breasts and her golden body
Shine, a protection for the saints.

Like her is Tārā – another lotus blossom
Of the East, a radiant garland of the luminous Good;
Mercy, in changing forms –
Yet present everywhere.
Let Thy Grace prevail.

Upāya, Prajnā

Yab-Yum: sie halten beide sich umschlungen,
Göttliche Kraft, göttlicher Geist; das heißt:
Upāya ist das Männliche, der Weg;
Weiblich ist Prajnā, der Erkenntnisgeist.

Doch gibt es eine andre Art, zu deuten:
Wahrheit ist männlich; weiblich ist das Trachten
Nach der Erleuchtung – lass dich, Schale, füllen,
Wie alle jene, die zum Licht erwachten.

Geistesgebiete

Wahrheit und Heiligkeit; Schönheit und Liebe;
Adel und Größe – Urtraum hoher Seelen.
Erst Ausgangspunkt, dann Ziel: im Lebenslauf
Soll sich entfalten, was im Herz wir wählen.

Und dann die Künste, die die Seel erfreuen:
Dichtung, Musik und Tanz; zum herben Wahren
Gehört das Schöne, Edle, das verjüngt –
So wie die Gopis Krishnas Freuden waren.

Baukunst, Gewandung, dann auch Kunstgewerbe,
Sind himmlisches Geschenk – ihr sollt sie pflegen
Mit wachem Geist, verstehend, was sie lehren;
Was nützt und schön ist – darauf ist der Segen!

Upāya, Prajnā

Yab-Yum: each holds the other in close embrace,
Divine Power and divine Spirit; this means:
Upāya is masculine, the Path;
Prajnā is feminine, the spirit of Wisdom.

But there is another way to interpret it:
Truth is masculine; striving for illumination
Is feminine — O cup, let thyself be filled,
As have all those who have awoken to the Light.

Domains of the Spirit

Truth and Holiness; Beauty and Love;
Nobility and Greatness — the primordial dream of lofty souls.
First starting-point, then goal: what we choose in our heart
Should unfold in the course of our life.

And then the arts that delight the soul:
Poetry, music and dance; to austere Truth
Belong the beautiful and the noble, which rejuvenate —
Just as the *gopīs* were Krishna's joy.

Architecture, dress, and craftsmanship too,
Are heavenly gifts — cultivate them
With a wakeful spirit, understanding what they teach.
What is useful and beautiful — upon them blessing rests.

Entartung

Ein altes Königsschloss ist schön an sich,
Jedoch der Innenprunk ist fürchterlich –
Es gibt nichts Überspanntres in der Welt.
Gelobt sei der Nomaden schlichtes Zelt!
Reichtum hat Sinn, wenn er zum Schönen fließt,
Nicht wenn er schwülen Traum in Formen gießt.

Barmherzigkeit: sie ziert des Reichen Herz;
Ergebenheit zieht Armut himmelwärts.
Armut hat Wert, wenn sie den Glauben nährt;
Wenn sie sich bitter gegen Reiche kehrt,
Ist ihr Verdienst dahin.
Ob reich, ob nicht –
Ihr stehet vor des Ewigen Gericht.

Ästhetik

Man sagte mir: Shrī Shánkara, der Jnānī,
War kein Ästhet; er blieb im strengen Kreise
Der Metaphysik. Schönheitsfragen waren
Ihm fremd. Er war und blieb der reine Weise.

Ihr Mathematiker, brecht nicht den Stab
Über den, der vom Schönen spricht. Die Weisen
Des Ostens predigten die Schönheit nicht,
Weil es in ihrer Welt nichts andres gab.

In alten Welten – und in jedem Land –
Ging Wahrheit und das Schöne Hand in Hand.

Degeneration

An ancient royal castle is beautiful in itself,
But the interior pomp is dreadful –
There is nothing more extravagant in the world.
Praised be the nomad's simple tent!
Richness has meaning when it flows toward beauty,
Not when it gives oppressive dreams a solid form.

Charity is the adornment of the rich man's heart;
Resignation draws the poor man heavenward.
Poverty has value when it nourishes faith;
When it turns bitterly against the rich,
Its merit is gone.
Whether rich or not –
Ye stand before the Judgment of Eternity.

Esthetics

Someone said to me that Shrī Shankara, the *jnānī*,
Was no esthete, that he remained within the strict realm
Of metaphysics, that questions of beauty were foreign
To him, that he was and remained the pure wise man.

Ye mathematicians, break not the rod
On him who speaks about the beautiful.
The wise men of the East did not preach beauty,
For in their world there was nothing else.

In the ancient worlds – and in every land –
Truth and the beautiful went hand in hand.

Bilderkunst

Was ist der Sinn von Statuen und Gemälden?
Teils Darstellung von dem, was wir gesehen,
Oder Magie; teils Bilder höchster Wesen,
Die herrschend über unsrem Schicksal stehen –

Sinn-Bilder, deren Nähe etwas bringt
Von Götterwesen, die herniedersteigen;
Und umgekehrt: die uns den Gnadenweg
Von unsrer Armut bis zum Himmel zeigen.

Auf andrer Ebne: Bilder sind nur da
Um wie ein Blumenstrauß ein Heim zu schmücken;
So mag zur kalten, harten Winterszeit
Ein Bild des Frühlings unsre Seel beglücken.

Entartung droht bei mancher Bilderkunst.
Auf Bilder will der Nahe Ost verzichten;
Abrahams Welt.
Gott weiß am besten, wie
Ein jedes Volk soll sein Gebet verrichten.

Tempora, Mores

Bildende Kunst: Neualtertum zerstörte
Was Mittelalters Weisheit treu behütet.
Barock: der wohl zum Schlechtesten gehörte
Was geistesleere Künstler je erbrütet.

Bewundert nicht der Baukunst kaltes Protzen,
Noch die Gemälde und ihr schwüles Strotzen.
Der Westen war von alledem besessen;
Gott helfe uns. Lasst uns den Kram vergessen.

Figurative Art

What is the meaning of statues and paintings?
Partly, representation of what we have seen,
Or magic; partly, images of highest beings
Who rule our destiny from above –

Symbols, whose nearness conveys something
Of divine beings who come down to earth;
And conversely: which show us the way of grace
From our poverty up to Heaven.

At another level, images are simply there
The way a bunch of flowers decorates a home;
So may, in the cold and harsh winter,
A picture of spring gladden the soul.

Degeneration threatens much figurative art.
The Near East wants to renounce images;
Abraham's world.
God knows best
How each people should perform its prayers.

Tempora, Mores

Visual art: the Renaissance destroyed
What the wisdom of the Middle Ages had faithfully protected.
Baroque: it belongs surely to the worst
That empty-minded artists ever hatched.

Admire not the cold ostentation of architecture,
Nor paintings with their sultry pomposity.
With all of this the West has been obsessed;
God help us. Let us forget the whole business.

Wohnkunst

Goldene Wandschirme Japans und Kakemonos –
Etwas vom Besten, das uns Künstler gaben.
Die düstern Ölgemälde, die Museen füllen –
Wer möchte sie in seinem Heime haben?

Sagt nicht, dies sei nicht wichtig. Innenräume
Wirken auf uns, gestalten unsre Träume.

Nichts was den Geist begünstigt ist zuviel –
Himmlische Offenbarung ist der Stil.

Tonsprache

Musik – sie drückt nicht nur Gefühle aus,
Sondern Mysterien auch, die uns belehren.
Wahrheit liegt in der Töne Sprachgewalt –
Die Frage ist, ob wir die Tiefe hören.

Im frühen Islam war Musik verpönt
Wegen der Weltlichkeit der meisten Leute.
Doch Rūmī brachte sie zu hoher Ehr
Weil sie als Gotteslieb sein Herz erfreute.

Tanzen

Ihr Körper ist die Landschaft reinen Seins,
Die Schönheit, Unschuld, Kindlichkeit verbindet;
Dann das Mysterium Werden, Tanz der Zeit,
Der Māyā durch den trunknen Leib verkündet.

Und dann der Klang der Trommel, der Musik:
Er hebt hervor die Form und ihr Bewegen,
Lässt gleichsam sie zerschmelzen in den Strom
Von Seligkeit, und so von Gottes Segen.

Art of the Dwelling-Place

Japanese golden screens and kakemonos –
Some of the best things that artists have given us.
The gloomy oil-paintings that fill museums –
Who would want to have them in his home?

Do not say, "this is not important". Interior spaces
Have an effect on us, they shape our dreams.

Nothing that favors the Spirit is superfluous –
The style is a heavenly revelation.

Language of Sounds

Music – it expresses not only feelings,
But also mysteries that instruct us.
Truth lies in the powerful language of sounds –
The question is whether we hear its depth.

In early Islam music was frowned upon
Because of the worldliness of most people.
But Rūmī brought it to highest honor
Because, as love of God, it delighted his heart.

Dancing

Her body is the landscape of pure Being,
Combining beauty, innocence and childlikeness;
Then the mystery of becoming, dance of time,
Proclaiming *Māyā* through the enraptured body.

And then the sound of drum, of music:
It emphasizes form and its movement,
Lets it, as it were, melt into the river
Of beatitude, and so of God's Blessing.

Der Künstler

Der wahre Künstler ist ein Werkzeug nur
Um kundzugeben Gott und die Natur –
Mysterien, die sich gnädig offenbaren,
Und die in Gottes Geist geschrieben waren.
Oder Magie: denn Zeichen können rufen
Was sie bedeuten in des Daseins Stufen.
Und dann: manchmal ist Kunst nur dies gewesen:
Bild einer Schönheit aus des Künstlers Wesen.

Nicht ist die Kunst nur in sich selbst begründet;
Noch ist sie, was verdorbner Geist erfindet.
Wer uns will Süße oder Größe schenken,
Der muss auch an den Sinn des Lebens denken.

Gartenkunst

Gezierte Gärten sollte es nicht geben;
Lasst doch die Pflanzen, wie sie wollen, leben.
Schaut auf die Wildnis: Schönres gibt es nicht
Vor Gottes schöpferischem Angesicht.

Zen-Gärten, statt zu blühn, philosophieren,
Und so des Gartens wahren Sinn verlieren.
Wollt ihr das Nichts darstellen, geht zum Strand
Des Meeres, und vergräbt den Geist im Sand.

The Artist

The true artist is but an instrument
To manifest God and nature –
Mysteries which graciously reveal themselves,
And which are inscribed in God's Spirit.
Or else magic: for signs can call forth
What they signify on different levels of existence.
And then, sometimes art is simply this:
An image of something beautiful in the artist's substance.

Art does not have its foundation solely within itself;
Nor is it what a depraved mind invents.
He who wants to give us sweetness or greatness
Must also think on the meaning of life.

The Art of Gardening

Artificial gardens should not exist;
Let the plants live as they wish.
Consider the wilderness: there is nothing more beautiful
Before the creative Face of God.

Zen gardens philosophize instead of blooming,
And so they lose the real meaning of gardening.
If you wish to depict the void, go to the seashore
And bury your mind in the sand!

II

Menschliches

Human Themes

Heilkunde

Heilkunst: sie soll des Menschen Leiden lindern,
Gar manches heilen, Übel auch verhindern;
Mag auch der Tod uns von der Erde raffen –
Ziel kann nicht sein, das Sterben abzuschaffen.

Die Medizin: sie kämpft – vielleicht gelingt es.
Sie ist ein Gut, und doch nichts Unbedingtes.
Lieber Schamanen, die uns wirklich heilen,
Als Ärzte, die den Leib zu Tode feilen.

Gesegnet sei, wer bei den Kranken weilt –
Nicht nur den Leib, wohl auch die Seele heilt.

Wissenschaft

„Ich nehme meine Zuflucht zu dem Herrn
Vor einem Wissen, das mir nutzlos ist.“
Dies sagte der Prophet. Frag die Gelehrten:
Was nützt euch, was ihr vom Antares wisst?

Astronomie – seid nicht zu dienstbeflissen;
Doch dass die Erde rund ist, dürft ihr wissen,
Denn es liegt nah und hat auch seinen Sinn;
Lasst die Andrómeda ins Nichts entfliehn.

The Art of Healing

The art of healing: it should alleviate suffering,
Heal many ailments, and also prevent ills;
Death can still wrench us away from this earth –
The aim cannot be to abolish dying.

Medicine: it battles – maybe it succeeds.
It is a good thing, and yet not absolute.
Rather shamans who really heal us,
Than doctors who polish the body to death.

Blessèd is he who stays with the sick –
He heals not only the body, but also the soul.

Science

"I take refuge in the Lord
From a knowledge that is of no use to me."
Thus said the Prophet. Ask the scientists:
What use is your knowledge of Antares to you?

Astronomy – do not be over zealous;
Of course you may know that the earth is round,
For this is obvious, and has its meaning;
But let Andromeda flee into the naught.

Eisernes Zeitalter

Von Mord und Totschlag träumt das Menschenvolk
Nun schon seit ein paar tausend wilden Jahren;
Doch früher nicht – so ändert sich die Zeit –
Weil früher Menschen keine Wölfe waren.

Im Kali-Yuga ist der Kampf Gesetz –
Shrī Krishna hat es feierlich gelehrt –
Denn wo die Missetaten sich verbreiten,
Braucht man den edlen Helden mit dem Schwert.

Vergesse nicht, gegen dich selbst zu streiten –
Kampf mit dem Drachen ist ein Geisteswert.

Ruhepunkte

Das Kali-Yuga ist nicht nur ein Fall
Hinab; an manchen Punkten steht es still:
Kosmische Werte können überall
Erscheinen, wenn der Allerhöchste will.

Es wirkt die Wahrheit und des Guten Macht;
Das Krita-Yuga schimmert durch die Nacht.

Dämmerung

Chaos im Wachstum buntgemischter Ahnen:
Rechnende Römer, träumende Germanen;
Der Kirche mystisch-weltliches Gesicht;
Launischer Modegeist, der vorwärts schwankte
Durch die Jahrhunderte – Ungleichgewicht:
Das war's, woran Europas Westen krankte.

Trotz alledem: da waren fromme Leute
Und Heilige – wie gestern, so auch heute.
Sonst Dämmrung überall. – „Es werde Licht!"

Iron Age

Humanity has dreamt of murder and slaughter
Already now for a few thousand wild years;
But earlier this was not so — times change —
Because men of earlier times were not like wolves.

In the *Kali-Yuga*, fighting is the law —
Shrī Krishna solemnly taught this —
For where misdeeds abound,
One needs the noble hero with his sword.

Do not forget to strive against thyself —
Fighting the dragon is a spiritual value.

Points of Rest

The *Kali-Yuga* is not only a fall
Downward; at certain points it stands still:
Cosmic values can appear everywhere,
If the All-Highest will.

Truth and the power of Good are at work;
The *Krita-Yuga* shimmers through the night.

Twilight

Chaos in the growth of highly diverse ancestors:
Calculating Romans, dreaming Germans;
The mystical-worldly face of the Church;
Capricious spirit of fashion, lurching forward
Through the centuries — lack of balance:
This is why Europe's West is ailing.

Despite everything, there have been pious people
And saints — as yesterday, so too today.
Otherwise, twilight everywhere. — "Let there be Light!"

Menschheitsfragen

Es gebe keine bösen Menschen – falsch
Ist diese Meinung, die auf Träumen fußt;
Es gebe böse Völker – ebenfalls
Ein Irrtum, unbewusste Rachelust.

Ein Mensch kann böse sein in seinem Grund,
Nicht weil Umstände ihn dazu verführen;
Ein Volk ist niemals tugendlos an sich –
Es kann nur zeitenweis den Kopf verlieren:
Ein Wahn mag eines Volkes Teil vergiften –
Ein schlechter Mensch kann all das Unheil stiften.

Im Mittelalter waren Sitten wild;
Die Heilgen passten dennoch in das Bild.
Und ohne Zweifel, Grausamkeit ist schändlich –
Sie ist im Menschen; sie ist unverständlich –
Es sei denn in der Metaphysik Kleid:
Sie ist ein Sandkorn der Allmöglichkeit.
Du magst es finden in den Heilgen Schriften –
Und niemand kann der Isis Schleier lüften.

Wenn eines Volkes Mehrheit gläubig ist,
Dann kann sie wie die Stimme Gottes sein.
Hingegen: trennt sie sich vom Glaubensgut,
Dann fällt sie auf ihr eignes Nichts herein.

Was nützet eitles Grübeln, eitle Klage?
„Sein oder Nichtsein – dies ist hier die Frage."

Human Questions

There are no bad human beings – false
Is this opinion, which rests upon dreams;
There are evil peoples – equally an error,
An unconscious desire for revenge.

A human being can be bad in his substance,
And not because circumstances lead him astray;
A people as such is never without virtue –
It can lose its head only for a time:
A mania may poison part of a people –
One wicked man can cause such a calamity.

In the Middle Ages customs were wild;
The saints were nonetheless part of the picture.
Without doubt, cruelty is shameful –
It is in man; it is incomprehensible –
Unless it be in metaphysical dress:
A grain of sand within All-Possibility.
Thou canst find it in the Holy Scriptures –
And no one can lift the veil of Isis.

When the majority of a people is believing,
Then the people can be like the voice of God.
Conversely: when it cuts itself off from the good of faith,
Then it falls away into its own nothingness.

What is the use of idle brooding or complaint?
"To be or not to be – that is the question."

Ideale

Die Jugendlichen haben Ideale;
Die Alten lächeln: „Mit des Alltags Sorgen
Wird's euch vergehn – des Lebens Ernst macht klug!"
Die Zeit verging. Klug bin ich nie geworden.

Ich blieb bei Wirklichkeiten, Idealen –
Ihr trinkt des Lebens Sinn aus leeren Schalen.

Schuldfrage

Verabendländert sind die Morgenländer –
So schrieb jemand – wenn sie an Unsinn glauben.
Wenn ohne westlich Gift sie weise sind,
Was lassen sie sich ihre Weisheit rauben?

Der Osten trägt nicht erste Schuld am Falle
Der Menschheit – jedoch Menschen sind wir alle!

Cogitatio

Bist du berühmt, wie andre vor dir waren –
Wer frägt nach dir in hunderttausend Jahren?

Bist du verachtet, wie so manche sind –
Was tut's, wenn dir der Herr ist wohlgesinnt?

„Alles ist eitel", sprach ein weiser König;
Er war mit Gott. – Der Welt Applaus ist wenig.

Ideals

Young people have ideals;
Old people laugh: "Come everyday responsibilities,
You will outgrow them – the seriousness of life makes one wiser!"
Time passed. And wiser I never became.

I stayed with my ideals, with realities –
Ye drink life's meaning out of empty cups.

A Question of Guilt

Orientals have been westernized –
So someone wrote – if they believe something foolish.
But if they were wise before the poison of the West,
Why did they let themselves be robbed of their wisdom?

The East does not bear the first guilt for the fall
Of humanity – but we are all human beings!

Cogitatio

If thou art famous, as others before thee were –
Who will ask after thee in a hundred thousand years?

If thou art despised, as so many are –
What does it matter, if the Lord is well-disposed toward thee?

"All is vanity," a wise king said;
He was with God. The world's applause is a small thing.

Wege

Hochmut beherrscht den Denker, dessen Hirn
Gespinste brütet und die Welt verdirbt.
Demütig ist des Glaubens treuer Knecht,
Des Laster in der Gottesliebe stirbt.
Und selbstlos ist der Weise, dessen Geist
Der allerhöchsten Wahrheit Licht erwirbt.

Verderbende Vernünftelei ist eines;
Und durchaus andres ist der Intellekt,
Des Herzens Schauen; dann der Glaubensweg,
Der Seelen tröstet und zum Heil erweckt.
Wenn du das, was dich in die Höhe zieht,
Gefunden, – hast du deinen Weg entdeckt.

Bedingung

Es ward gesagt: des Höchsten Name rettet,
Trotz unsrer Sünden drückenden Gewichts;
Wahrheit! Indessen: dem gemeinen Menschen
Nützet die Anrufung des Namens nichts.

Gott hat es mit der Wunderkraft nicht eilig;
Und nur die edlen Seelen macht er heilig.
Dem Namen zu soll man mit Ehrfurcht streben:
„Ihr sollt das Heilige nicht Hunden geben!“

Seid schlicht mit Gott – Er hört euch. Jedoch auch:
Edlen Gemüts! Dies will des Himmels Brauch.

Paths

Pride dominates the thinker whose brain
Hatches delusions and corrupts the world.
The true servant of faith is humble,
His vices perish in the love of God.
And selfless is the sage, whose mind
Attains the light of Highest Truth.

Corruptive sophistry is one thing;
The Intellect, heart's vision, is quite other;
Then there is the path of faith, that brings
Solace to souls and awakens them to salvation.
When thou hast found what draws thee upward,
Thou hast discovered thy Path.

Condition

It has been said: the Supreme Name saves us,
Despite the crushing weight of our sins;
True! However, to a base human being
The invocation of the Name is of no avail.

God does not hasten with miraculous powers;
Only noble souls does He make holy.
One should approach the Name with awe:
"Ye should not give what is sacred to dogs."

Be simple before God — He hears you. But also:
Be of noble mind! Heaven's way requires it.

Audiatur

Audiatur et altera pars – eine Regel aus Gold:
Höret auf beide Parteien, so ihr Gerechtigkeit wollt.
Ausnahme ist es gewiss, wenn einer von beiden
Wahrlich ein Narr oder Schuft ist, welchen zu meiden
Recht der Natur ist. Des Ehrenmanns Zeugnis genügt.
Scheltet den Hitzkopf, wenn er die Wahrheit verbiegt.

Menschen sollen sich achten. Das Recht soll gewinnen,
Doch schaut auf das Wesen der Dinge und bleibet bei Sinnen.
Friede ist heilig – ein Schatz, der von obenher kam;
Fürchtet den Herrn, und begrüßt euch. Alaikum Salām.

Magnificat

Maria und Elisabeth: sie trafen
Und grüßten sich; die Heilge Jungfrau sprach,
Vom Geist erfüllt: „Der Herr hat mich erwählt;
Man wird mich selig preisen. Demut ist
Der Herzen Zier: klein sein vor Gottes Größe.
Er sättiget den Armen; doch den Reichen,
Er lässt ihn gehn.“ – Was ist damit gemeint?
Reich ist, wer keinen Raum hat für den Herrn
In seinem Herzen, weil die Welt es füllt.
O Mensch, sieh zu, dass eine heilge Leere
Des allerhöchsten Namens Fülle ehre.

Maria – voll der Gnad. Gott sei gelobt,
Der durch die Demut unser Herz erprobt.

Audiatur

Audiatur et altera pars – a golden rule:
Listen to both parties if you seek justice.
An exception, of course, is when one of the two
Is really a fool or a scoundrel, whom to avoid
Is a natural right. The honest man's testimony suffices.
Chastise the hothead if he distorts the truth.

Men should respect one another. The right should win,
But look at the nature of things, and don't lose your head.
Peace is sacred – a treasure from above;
Fear the Lord and greet one another. *Alaikum salām.*

Magnificat

Mary and Elizabeth: they met and greeted each other;
The blessèd Virgin spoke, filled with the Holy Ghost,
And said: "The Lord has chosen me;
They shall call me blessed. Humility
Is the heart's adornment: to be small before God's greatness.
He fills the poor, but the rich
He turns away." What does this mean?
"Rich" is he who has no room for the Lord
In his heart, because it is filled with the world.
O man, see that a holy emptiness
Honor the fullness of the Supreme Name.

Mary – full of Grace. Praise be to God,
Who tests our hearts through humility.

Caritas

Du, der du einsam betest, denke nicht
Du seist allein; auch andern gegenüber,
Die du nicht kennst, ist dein Gebet ein Gut
Und eine Segenskraft und eine Pflicht.

Gottesgedenken schuldest du dem Höchsten –
Und dann dir selbst, und ebenso dem Nächsten.

Der Ort, wo für den Herrn ihr stillesteht,
Ist wie ein Pol, um den die Welt sich dreht.

Das Schwert

Lass der Wahrheit lichtes Schwert durchschneiden
Nebelschleier deiner dunklen Seele;
Wort des Allerhöchsten und des Heiles –
Trag es stets im Herzen, in der Kehle.

Denke nicht, des Menschen Seel sei heilig
Wenn sie töricht jeden Kampf vermiede;
Den gerechten Kämpfer sollst du ehren,
Denn im edlen Schwerte wohnt der Friede.

Deine Waffe – dies sei wohl verstanden –
Soll nicht eilig eitlen Streit entzünden;
Lass sie mit des Guten Feinde kämpfen,
Falschen Frieden weise überwinden.

Caritas

Thou who prayest in solitude, think not
Thou art alone; for others too,
Whom thou knowest not, thy prayer is a good
And a benediction and a duty.

God-remembrance thou owest to the Most High,
Then to thyself, and likewise to thy neighbor.

The place where ye stand still before the Lord
Is like a pole round which the world is turning.

The Sword

Let truth's bright sword cut through
The veils of fog in thy dark soul;
The Word of the All-Highest and of salvation –
Carry it always in thy heart and on thy tongue.

Do not think man's soul is holy
When it foolishly avoids every fight;
Thou shouldst give honor to the just warrior,
For peace dwells in the noble sword.

Thy weapon – understand this well –
Should not kindle rash and needless conflict.
Let it battle the enemy of the good,
And wisely overcome false peace.

Das Entscheidende

Des Menschen Wert beruht auf seiner Würde,
Auf seinem Sein vor Gott, nicht auf dem Machen;
Der Stadtmensch, der in hohen Häusern wohnt,
Soll nicht den, der in Hütten lebt, verlachen.

Des Menschen Wert ist seine Einstellung
Zum Unbedingten, nicht sein Wo und Wie –
Ob er nun Kunst und Wissenschaft erzeugt,
Oder den Büffel jagt auf der Prärie.

Die Welt ist Sinnbild, wie sie auch erscheine –
Wirklichkeit ist allein das Große Eine.

Nicht vergessen

Freude an Gott – wie soll ich's euch erklären?
Ihr sollt euch nicht so leicht bedrücken lassen,
An eitlen Bildern und Gedanken zehren,
Dumpf trabend durch des Alltags graue Gassen.

Seid dankbar: Menschsein ist das größte Glück –
Ist nicht der Mensch das Tor zum Himmelreich?
Ihr habt die höchste Wahrheit, das Gebet –
Und Gottes Gnade macht euch Engeln gleich.

What is Decisive

Man's worth lies in his dignity,
In his being before God, not in his doing;
The city-dweller who lives in tall houses
Should not scoff at the one who dwells in huts.

Man's worth is in his attitude
Toward the Absolute, not his where and how –
Whether he is an artist or a scientist,
Or a hunter of buffalo on the prairie.

The world is a symbol, however it may seem –
The Great One alone is Reality.

Do Not Forget

Joy in God – how shall I explain it?
You should not let yourselves be so easily weighed down,
Nor feed on idle images and thoughts,
Trudging wearily down the grey alleys of everyday.

Be thankful: to be man is the greatest good fortune –
Is not man the gate to Heaven's Kingdom?
You have the highest Truth, and you have prayer –
And God's grace makes you like unto the angels.

Absicht

Soll man denn Stund für Stund an Gott nur denken –
Ein Schwacher, Kranker, kann es nicht erzwingen.
Doch heißt es: Engel sprechen das Gebet
An seiner Stell; so kann das Werk gelingen.

Lieber mit einer reinen Absicht sterben
Als alles durch den eitlen Schein verderben.
Die Absicht ist der Kern, der Punkt zum i –
Was jenseits unsrer Kraft, verlangt Gott nie.

Greise

Im Greisenalter – hat jemand geschrieben –
Sei man von allem Äußeren getrennt;
Gleichgültig sei das ganze Außenleben –
Der nahe Tod sei alles, was man kennt.

Ich bin im hohen Alter, doch die Welt
Ist für mich stets die gleiche Welt geblieben;
Und so die Seele, die im Wahren lebt –
Was kommen wird, ist was zutiefst wir lieben.

Intention

Must one then, hour after hour, think only on God?
A weak and ailing person cannot force this.
But it is said that angels say the prayer
In their stead; and so the work can succeed.

Better to die with a pure intention
Than spoil everything through empty show.
Intention is the kernel, the dot on the "i" –
God never demands what is beyond our strength.

The Aged

In old age – someone wrote –
One is separated from outward things;
All outward life becomes indifferent –
Approaching death is all one knows.

I have reached a ripe old age, yet the world
Has remained always the same world for me;
So also the soul, which lives in the True –
What will come, is what we most profoundly love.

Größe

Nicht ist die Größe von der Welt,
Sie liegt im Gottgedenken.
Verdienst wächst nicht auf deinem Feld,
Lass Gott dir Gnade schenken.

Wohn still in deines Herzens Haus
Abseits der vielen hundert;
Was nützet dir der Welt Applaus
Wenn Gott dich nicht bewundert?

Es steht geschrieben: Gott ist groß.
Was kümmern dich die Leute?
Verharre in der Gnade Schoß –
Wie gestern, so auch heute.

Die Stimme

Der Weise soll den Suchenden belehren –
Er möcht sich innerlich vor Gram verzehren
In dieser Welt. Doch dann kommt mildes Wort
Vom Himmel her: was deine Welt auch sei,
Der Friede naht, der Albdruck geht vorbei –

Denn vincit omnia Veritas. Das Rechte
War vor dem Trug; es nahen Gottes Mächte.
Und dies ist einer Heilgen Schrift entnommen:
„Wahrlich, nach Schwerem wird das Leichte kommen" –
Was eitler Erdentrug zuvor auch brächte.

Greatness

Greatness is not of the world,
It lies in God-remembrance.
Merit does not grow in thy field,
Let God bestow grace on thee.

Dwell in stillness in the house of thy heart,
Apart from the crowd of many;
What profits thee the world's applause,
If God does not approve thee?

It is written: God is great.
Why should people trouble thee?
Abide thou in the lap of grace –
As yesterday, so too today.

The Voice

The wise man is supposed to teach the seeker –
Inwardly he may be consumed with grief
In this world. But then comes a gentle word
From Heaven: whatever thy world may be,
Peace approaches, the nightmare goes away –

For *vincit omnia Veritas.* The Right existed
Before illusion; God's powers approach.
And this is taken from a sacred scripture:
"Verily, after hardship cometh ease" –
Whatever idle earth-deceit may have brought before.

Nixen

Nixen bezaubern Fischer mit Gesang
Und ziehn sie in die kühle, grüne Tiefe –
So folgt der Weltmensch seiner Leidenschaft,
Als ob ihn eine süße Stimme riefe.

Der Weltliche; nicht so der Geistesmann,
Der alles liebt in Gott, nicht ohne Ihn.
Durchsichtig ist das Gute in der Welt;
Und Gott ist aller Dinge letzter Sinn.

Sag nicht, dass edle Schönheit uns betört –
Nicht den, der ihres Sanges Tiefe hört.

Kleinigkeiten

Groß sein, und doch auf kleine Dinge achten:
Gar oft ist Kleines wie ein Teil der Größe.
Der Eitle mag die Kleinigkeit verachten –
Der Kluge muss den Sinn des Kleinen sehen.

Groß sein ist nicht die Kunst, sich aufzublähen –
Größe will nach der Dinge Wesen trachten.

Mermaids

Mermaids bewitch fishermen with songs,
And pull them into the cool, green depths –
Thus the worldly man follows his passions,
As if called by a sweet voice.

The worldly man; not the spiritual man,
Who loves all things in God, and not without Him.
The good in the world is transparent;
And God is the ultimate meaning of all things.

Say not that noble beauty beguiles us –
Not those who hear the depth of its song.

Little Things

To be great, and yet pay heed to little things:
Quite often the little is like a part of greatness.
The vain person may scorn what is small –
The one who is intelligent must see its meaning.

To be great is not the art of puffing oneself up –
Greatness strives toward the essence of things.

Wünsche

Man kann nicht völlig ohne Wünsche sein
Wenn man ein Mensch ist. Denn der Mensch muss essen
Und trinken um zu leben. Doch man kann
Die Dinge wünschen und nicht Gott vergessen –
Sonst käm kein Segen auf den Erdenplan.

Man kann sich etwas wünschen ohne Gier –
Man weiß, das Irdische hat seine Grenzen,
So wie wir selbst. Man soll kein Erdending
Mit Anbetung und Eichenlaub bekränzen –
Neben dem Schöpfer ist die Welt gering.

Du sollst dein Herz nicht ganz ans Halbe heften;
Denn: „Liebe Gott mit allen deinen Kräften."

Timor

Jemand behauptet, er sei Gottes Freund
Und brauche keine Furcht. Falsch ist dies ganz;
Gott liebt nicht Übermut – Er nimmt nicht an,
Dass man sich schmücke mit der Freundschaft Kranz.

Furcht ohne Liebe gibt es, dies ist klar;
Doch ohne Fürchten gibt es keine Liebe.
Denn Hochachtung ist aller Liebe Preis –
Ansonsten nichts von Minne übrig bliebe.

Desires

One cannot be wholly without desires,
Being human; for man must eat and drink
In order to live. Yet one can
Desire things without forgetting God –
Otherwise no blessing would come to the earthly plane.

One can desire something without greed –
One knows that what is earthly has its limits,
As we ourselves have. One should not crown
An earthly thing with worship and with laurels –
Beside the Creator, the world is slight.

Do not fix thy whole heart on what is but a part;
For: "Love the Lord thy God with all thy might."

Timor

Someone says that he is God's friend
And need not fear. This is entirely false;
God loves not pride – He does not accept
That man should confer upon himself the garland of friendship.

Fear without love exists, this is evident;
But without fear there is no love,
For reverence is the price of all love –
Otherwise nothing of love would remain.

Ein Mangel

Ein arges Übel ist die Kleinlichkeit;
Der Durchschnittsmensch hat keine Seelengröße
Und kann nicht wissen, wie der Edle fühlt –
Wie er erlebt die Lust, des Schicksals Stöße;

Wie er der Dinge Sinn und Tiefe schaut,
Das Fatum annimmt und auf Gott vertraut.

Widerschein

Größe ist Gottes. Doch der Größe Schein
Kann durch die Gnade auch im Menschen sein.

Nie hat ein großer Mensch sein Wort gebrochen;
Größe ist halten, was man hat versprochen.

Ob hohes Wort, ob Bänkelsängerei –
Schau zu, dass Gottes Wahrheit drinnen sei!

Treue

Treu ist der edle Mensch. Treulos der Schlechte –
Selbst gute Dinge machen ihm Beschwerden
Sowie sie dauern. Nicht so der Gerechte:
Er kann nicht edler Dinge müde werden.

Selbstsucht und eitle Oberflächlichkeit –
Der Tor sucht und bewundert, was ihm neu.
Großmut und Tiefe wollen Lieb und Treu –

Das Edle gründet in der Ewigkeit.

A Defect

Pettiness is a serious malady;
The average man has no greatness of soul
And cannot know how the noble man feels –
How he experiences pleasure, or the blows of fate;

How he looks on the meaning and depth of things,
Accepts his destiny and trusts in God.

Reflection

Greatness belongs to God. But its reflection
Can, through grace, also be in man.

Never has a great man broken his word;
Greatness is to keep what one has promised.

Whether lofty words or simple ballads –
See to it that they contain God's Truth.

Faithfulness

The noble man is faithful. Faithless is the bad –
Even good things are a burden for him
Whilst they last. Not so the just man:
He cannot tire of noble things.

Self-seeking and vain superficiality –
The fool seeks and admires what is new.
Magnanimity and depth want love and faithfulness –

What is noble is rooted in Eternity.

Fātihah

Mohammedaner beten: „Führe uns
Den graden Pfad; derer, die dein Erbarmen
Beschützt; nicht derer, die dein Zornesblitz
Wird treffen; auch nicht der Verführten, Armen,

Die auf dem Irrweg sind.“ – Dies betet jeder;
Warum? Weil jedem Herzen Hochmut droht;
Und dann, weil jede Seele irren kann –
Hochmut und Irrtum sind des Menschen Not.

Und der Pfad jener, die Erbarmen finden?
Des Menschen Urbild könnte es verkünden –
Demut und Wahrheit: deines Strebens Grund –
Von frühsten Jahren bis zur letzten Stund.

Ekstasis

Verzückung schließt das Weltbewusstsein aus;
Vergessen ist der Leib, der Seele Haus.
Dies ist schon viel – doch alles ist es nicht;
Noch andre Werte fallen ins Gewicht.

Ekstase – sagen einige – verwerfe
Den Außentrug. Gewisslich; und was weiter?
Das Allererste ist Erkenntnisschärfe;
Verzückung macht den Menschen nicht gescheiter.

Das Urgebet ist der Ekstase Form;
Samādhi schließt nicht aus des Lebens Norm.
Heilig ist nicht, wer auf ein Wunder harrt,
Sondern wer weiß von Gottes Gegenwart.

Du kannst der Außenwelt Beachtung schenken –
Das Höchste ist das reine Gottgedenken.
Der Weise, den kein Seelentrug bedrückt,
Ist stets durch Gottes Gegenwart beglückt.

Fātihah

Muslims pray: "Lead us on the straight path;
The path of those whom Thy mercy protects,
Not of those whom Thy wrath's thunderbolt will strike,
Nor of the poor souls that are led astray

And walk the path of error." — This everyone prays;
And why? Because pride threatens every heart;
And then, because every soul can err —
Pride and error are the misery of mankind.

And the path of those who find Mercy?
Man's archetype can tell of it —
Humility and Truth: the foundation of thy striving —
From thine earliest years until the final hour.

Ekstasis

Rapture excludes consciousness of the world;
Forgotten is the body, the soul's house.
This is already much — yet it is not everything;
Other values also have importance.

Ecstasy — some say — casts off
Outward illusion. Certainly; and what next?
The very first thing is keenness of discernment;
Rapture does not make a man more intelligent.

Quintessential prayer is the framework for ecstasy;
Samādhi does not exclude the norms of life.
Holy is not he who waits for a miracle,
But he who is conscious of the Presence of God.

Thou canst give attention to the outside world —
But the highest thing is pure God-remembrance.
The wise man, whom no soul-illusion weighs down,
Is forever made happy through God's Presence.

Tadel

Ein Mystizismus, der Gefühl allein
Als Weg zum Höchsten Gute gelten lässt,
Und Dummheit irgendwie als Demut preist –
Ist süßer Trug. Halt du am Wahren fest!

Verwerfung aller Glaubensgrenzen ist
Noch lang nicht Weisheit. Sind wir alle Brüder?
Großmut ist anders als Gleichmacherei –
Gefühl mag lügen. Wahrheit, komme wieder!

Bescheidenheit

Die Affen wollten Menschen sein, die Tiere;
So sind sie Parias vor des Tempels Türe.
Und so die Menschen, die sich übersteigern –
Gott wird dem Ehrgeiz jede Kron verweigern.

Man kann die Kleinheit nicht zur Größe biegen –
Doch in Bescheidenheit kann Größe liegen.

Blame

A mysticism that values sentiment alone
As the way to the Sovereign Good,
And praises stupidity as if it were humility –
This is sweet illusion. Cling to the True!

The rejection of all confessional narrowness
Is still a long way from wisdom. Are we all brothers?
Magnanimity is not the same as egalitarianism –
Feelings may lie. O Truth, come back!

Modesty

Monkeys – animals – wanted to be human beings;
So they are pariahs before the temple door.
And so are men who overstep themselves –
God will refuse every crown to ambition.

One cannot twist littleness into greatness –
But greatness can reside in modesty.

Vier Pfeiler

Ergebenheit: annehmen, was Gott will;
Vertrauen: glauben, dass Gott Güte strahlt.
Beides beruht auf Wollen und Gefühl –
Es ist für jeden Menschen, jung und alt.

Erhabenheit: die Welt von Oben sehen,
Sodass man gleichsam auf den Wolken geht.
Gewissheit: mit des Herzens Auge schauen,
Das aller Dinge tiefen Grund versteht.

Nicht jeder Mensch kann reinen Geist erreichen;
Doch jeder kann verstehn des Glaubens Zeichen.
Der Glaube gibt fürs Heil genügend Licht –
Doch Weisheit ohne Seele gibt es nicht.

Das Auge

Ein Auge, das sich öffnet und sich schließt –
So ist das Leben, das euch endlos scheint.
Es strahlt vor Glück, und seine Träne fließt –
Es gibt kein Auge, das noch nie geweint.

Das Auge schauet in die Welt hinein –
Möge des Lebens Blick das Wahre sehen,
Den Gegensatz von Nichts und Licht verstehen –
Möge dein Aug auf Gott gerichtet sein!

Four Pillars

Resignation: accepting what God wills;
Trust: believing that God radiates goodness.
Both are founded on will and sentiment –
They are for every man, both young and old.

Serenity: seeing the world from above,
As if one were walking on the clouds.
Certitude: seeing with the eye of the heart,
Which understands the deep essence of all things.

Not every man can reach the pure Spirit,
But everyone can understand the signs of faith.
Faith gives light sufficient for salvation –
But wisdom without soul does not exist.

The Eye

An eye that opens and then closes –
Such is the life that seems endless to thee.
It shines with happiness, and its tears flow –
No eye exists that never wept.

The eye looks deeply into the world –
So may life's gaze perceive the True, and understand
The opposition between nothingness and Light –
May thine eye direct its gaze toward God!

Glaube und Dank

Unglaube ist im Grunde, zu vergessen:
Vergänglich ist der eitle Erdenkram;
Und Undank ist es, nicht mehr zu ermessen,
Wie viele Gnade uns vom Himmel kam.

Es muss so sein auf Erden: man muss kämpfen;
Glaube und Dank – sie werden Leiden dämpfen.
„Die Wahrheit kam, das Eitle ist zerstoben –
Wahrlich, das Eitle ist aus Nichts gewoben."

Suum cuique

Ausdehnungen: Raum und Zeit und Form und Zahl –
So gibt es in der Seel verschiedne Welten:
Verstand und Liebe, Willenstätigkeit –
Ein Standort sollte nicht den andern schelten.

Denn jede Welt ist irgendwie für sich,
Und doch nicht einzig, denn wir sind gebaut
Aus Ausdehnungen, und sind dennoch eins.

Wohl dem, der allerorts das Wahre schaut.

Rückblick

Ein Schleier vor des Seelenkerns Gesicht,
Gewoben aus den Dingen, die geschehen –
Man muss wohl alt sein, um es klar zu sehen;
Jugend mag es verstehn, doch sieht es nicht –
Und eingefroren sind die meisten Greise.

Zeitlos und ohne Alter ist der Weise.

Faith and Gratitude

Unbelief is, at bottom, to forget
That idle earthly din is transient;
And ingratitude is no longer to realize
How many graces come to us from Heaven.

On earth it must be so: one must struggle;
Faith and gratitude – they will allay suffering.
"Truth has come, vanity is dispelled –
Verily, vanity is woven of nothingness."

Suum cuique

Dimensions: space and time and form and number –
Likewise in the soul there are different worlds:
Reason and love, the will's activity –
One standpoint should not reproach the other.

For each world is somehow unto itself,
And yet is not unique, for we are fashioned
Of dimensions, and yet are one.

Blessèd is he who sees the True in every place.

Looking Back

A veil before the face of the soul's deep core,
Woven of the things that have happened –
One must be old indeed to see it clearly;
Youth may understand, but does not see it –
And amongst the old, most are frozen.

The sage is timeless and without age.

La Vida

La vida es sueño, schrieb ein Spanier einst –
Gleichviel, Mensch, ob du lachest oder weinst.
Ruhe im Herrn, lass Ihn dein Schicksal weben –
Dein ist der Traum, und Gottes ist das Leben.

Muero porque no muero – denn das Sterben
In Gott heißt Gottes ewges Leben erben.

Sünde

Was soll der Sünder tun nach seiner Sünde
Auf dass sie nicht des Höchsten Zorn entzünde?
Er muss den Trug erkennen und bereuen
Und umso bessre Werke um sich streuen –
Und dann vor Gott die strenge Lehre ziehen.
Wer so bereut, dem hat der Herr verziehen.

Die strenge Lehre: denn es geht aufs Ganze.
Du kannst vor Gott auf halbem Weg nicht weilen;
Bist du gefallen, höher musst du streben –
Du musst dem Ewigen entgegen eilen.
Du kennst das Gleichnis vom verlornen Sohn:
Groß war die Sünd, größer des Strebens Lohn.

Tu einen Schritt – heißt es – auf Gottes Wegen:
Der Höchste eilet dir zehn Schritt entgegen.

La Vida

La vida es sueño, a Spaniard once wrote –
No matter, O man, whether thou laugh or weep.
Repose in the Lord, let Him weave thy destiny –
Thine is the dream, thy life belongs to God.

Muero porque no muero – for dying in God
Means to inherit God's eternal Life.

Sin

What should the sinner do after his sin,
In order not to kindle the wrath of the Most High?
He must recognize his error and regret it,
And sow better works around him –
Then draw the stern lesson before God.
The one who thus regrets, the Lord has forgiven him.

The lesson is stern because it goes the whole way.
Before God, thou canst not stop at half;
If thou hast fallen, thou must strive higher –
Thou must hasten towards the Eternal.
Thou know'st the parable of the prodigal son:
Great was his sin, greater the reward for his striving.

Take one step – it is said – on the Lord's Path:
The Most High will hasten ten steps towards thee.

Leiden

Der Mensch muss sich mit seinem Los bescheiden:
Da sind die Kranken, die durch Jahre leiden;
Sie sind gesondert, sind in Gottes Huld –
Ihr Weg zu Gott ist Glaube und Geduld.

Was ist denn unsre arme Erdenzeit
Verglichen mit des Himmels Ewigkeit!
Der Herrgott rechnet ihnen keine Schuld –
„Wahrlich, das Leichte kommt nach allem Leid.“

Fortuna

Tu, was der Leib im Alltagsleben braucht,
Und tu, was Segen in der Welt bewirkt;
Geh des Gebetes Weg, der Heil verbürgt,
Und Gottes Frieden in die Seele haucht.

Der Mensch strebt nach dem Glück, indess er weiß
Dass in Vergänglichkeit die Dinge münden;
Und mancher glaubt, Glück sei im Erdenkreis;
Findet er's nicht in Gott, er wird's nicht finden.

Höhe und Tiefe

Gottesbewusstsein – Gegenwart des Lichts.
Die Welt – sie ist ein Hin und Her, vielleicht
Mit Größe; oder kleiner Lärm um nichts,
Der nie von unsrer Seele Schwelle weicht.

Gottesbewusstsein: kann man es beschreiben
Mit einem Bilde, das man nie vergisst?
Ein Glück in ungestörter, weißer Höhe;
In einer Tiefe, wo kein Fragen ist.

Suffering

One must be content with one's lot:
There are sick people who suffer year after year;
They are set apart, they are in God's favor —
Their way to God is faith and patience.

What, after all, is our poor earthly term
Compared with the eternity of Heaven!
The Lord God lays no blame on them —
"Verily after all suffering cometh ease."

Fortuna

Do what the body needs in daily life,
And do what brings blessings to the world;
Walk the path of prayer, which ensures salvation,
And breathes God's Peace into the soul.

Man longs for happiness, yet well he knows
That things flow into ephemerality;
Happiness, some think, lies in the earthly sphere;
If they find it not in God, they will not find it.

Height and Depth

God-consciousness — a presence of Light.
The world — it is a to-and-fro, perhaps
With greatness; or else a little noise about nothing,
That never leaves the threshold of our soul.

God-consciousness: can one describe it
With an image never to be forgotten?
A happiness on a white, untroubled height;
And in a depth, where no questions are.

Religionen

Die Religionen seien überflüssig –
So denken manche, die nur Äußres sehen.
Doch unentbehrlich ist die Religion,
Auf dass die Leut auf Gottes Boden stehen.

Innerlichkeit: dies ist das große Wort.
Der Mensch muss eine wahre Seele haben,
Ein Selbst und eine Mitte; lasst ihn nicht
Wie Tiere durch ihr armes Leben traben.

Sagt nicht, die Dogmen widersprechen sich;
Denn nur des Glaubens Frucht ist wesentlich.

Glaube und Gnosis

Die Religion – ein kosmisches Phänomen,
Und so die Heiligkeit, die Wunder wirkt;
Anders begründet ist die Gnosis, die
So wie der Glaubensweg das Heil verbürgt,
Durch andres Denken und auf andre Weise –
Doch beide sind im selben Segenskreise.

Erschaffen ist der Intellectus nicht;
Und unerschaffen ist des Sufi Licht.
Der Allerhöchste kennt sein eigen Wesen
Im Weisen wohnend, den Er auserlesen.

Religions

Religions are superfluous –
So think some, who see only the outside.
Yet religion is indispensable,
So that the people may stand on God's ground.

Inwardness: this is the great word.
Man must possess a truthful soul,
A self and a center; let him not trot
As animals do through their poor life.

Say not the dogmas contradict each other;
For only the fruit of faith is essential.

Faith and Gnosis

Religion – a cosmic phenomenon,
And so is holiness, which can work miracles;
Gnosis is grounded differently,
It guarantees salvation, like the path of faith,
But through other thinking, and in another way –
Yet the same circle of blessing contains them both.

The Intellect is not created,
And uncreated is the Sufi's Light.
The Most High recognizes His own Essence
Dwelling in the sage whom He has chosen.

Ratio

Kann die Vernunft Allmöglichkeit begreifen?
Das bloße Denken ist sich nicht im Klaren.
Das Herz muss Höchstem Sein entgegenreifen
Um rein zu werden, das zu offenbaren,
Was es im Grunde ist: der Gottheit Schauen.

Der Seele Weg ist Demut und Vertrauen.

Dhikr

„Verflucht hat Gott die Erdenwelt
Mit allem, was ihr Raum enthält –
Ausnahme ist das Gottgedenken,
Und Dinge, die zu ihm uns lenken."

So der Prophet. Nur das ist gut,
Des Wesen in das Wahre mündet;
Gesegnet sei der Liebe Glut,
Wenn sie uns tief mit Gott verbindet.

Ratio

Can reason grasp All-Possibility?
Mere thinking does not see it clearly.
The heart must ripen toward the Highest Being
In order to become pure, and to manifest
What it is in its essence: vision of the Godhead.

The soul's path is humility and trust.

Dhikr

"God has cursed the earthly world
And all its space contains –
Save only God-remembrance,
And things that lead us to it."

Thus spake the Prophet. Only that is good
Whose nature flows into the True;
Blessèd be the ardor of love
When it binds us deeply to God.

Kleinglaube

Gläubig ist nicht, wer nur an Gott nicht zweifelt;
Gläubig ist der, dem Gott die Mitte ist.
Für viele ist Gott bloß der Hintergrund
Zu einem Leben, das ins Nichts zerfließt.

So gab es große Dichter, deren Leier
Erschuf die allerschönste Melodie;
Doch nur zum träumen, andre zu bezaubern —
Vergebnes Leben, und vergebne Müh.

Man soll nicht Perlen in die Asche streuen —
Das Erdenleben kann man Besserm weihen.
Nicht, dass der Herr die Torheit nie verzieh —
Wohl mancher mocht sich Gottes Großmut freuen.

Credo

Der Glaube schenkt uns heilge Wahrheit ein;
Die Wahrheit schenket uns des Glaubens Wein.
Intelligo ut credam, könnt man sagen —
Ein Glaube kann den andern überragen.

Zunächst ist Glaube: fühlen, Gott muss sein;
Sodann: der Gottheit Selbstsein in sich tragen.

Little Faith

A believer is not he who merely has no doubts about God;
A believer is the one for whom God is the Center.
For many God is merely the background
To a life that flows away into nothingness.

Thus there were great poets whose lyres
Created the most beautiful melodies;
But only to dream and to enchant others –
A futile life, and a futile effort.

One should not cast pearls into the ashes –
One can dedicate earthly life to something better.
Not that the Lord has never forgiven foolishness –
Many a one has benefited from God's Magnanimity.

Credo

Faith pours out for us the sacred Truth;
Truth pours out for us the wine of faith.
Intelligo ut credam, one could say –
One mode of faith can exceed the other.

First there is faith: to feel that God must be;
And then: to bear the divine Selfhood within oneself.

Randbemerkung

Wahrheiten darf die Feder wiederholen;
Auf gleiche Weise sind sie nie gesagt.
Es ist, als wollt ich neue Antwort geben –
Als hätte mich in mir ein Geist befragt.

Ob Einmal oder Mehrmal euch gefällt –
Ein wahres Wort ist eine ganze Welt.
Auch Schönheit: lasst sie mehrmals wiederkehren;
Denn jede Blume kann uns neu belehren.

Verstehet wohl: die Feder kommt von Drüben,
Und was der Himmel will, das wird geschrieben.

Worte

Kein Zweifel, dass des Menschen Wort vergeht,
Wie alles, was von dieser Erde ist;
Doch wähnet nicht, es sei vom Wind verweht,
Wenn es aus geisterfüllter Feder fließt –

Wenn in den Sternen es geschrieben steht.

Marginal Remark

The pen has the right to repeat truths;
They are never expressed in the same way.
It is as if I wished to give new answers –
As if a spirit inside me had asked a question.

Whether you prefer it once or several times –
A true word is a whole universe.
And so is beauty: let it return again and again,
For every flower can teach us anew.

Understand well: the pen comes from Beyond,
And what Heaven wills, shall be written.

Words

Without a doubt, man's words pass away,
Like everything that is of this earth;
But do not think that they are swept off by the wind
When they flow from a pen filled with the Spirit –

When they stand written in the stars.

III

Urlehre

Primordial Doctrine

Der Augenblick

Seltsam, wenn man vergleicht die Zeitlichkeit
Mit dem Mysterienland der Ewigkeit:
Was gibt uns Recht, den Augenblick zu lieben?
Ein Ewiges, von einem heilgen Drüben.

Ein erstes Ding ist des Besitzes Glück –
Ein andres, des Erlebens Jetzigkeit;

Ein drittes geht auf Gottes Sein zurück.

Innewerden

Der Tag, die Nacht; Vollmond, Neumond, das Jahr –
Sommer und Winter, wie es immer war.
Zenith und Nadir, Nord, Süd, Ost und West –
So ist die Welt beschaffen, weit und fest.
Der Raum, das Zeitrad; kosmisches Gedicht –
Der Isis Tanz. Ihr Antlitz seht ihr nicht.

Und dann? Dies soll euch nicht des Muts berauben –
Denn „selig, die nicht sehen und doch glauben."
Des Weisen Blick ist Schauen und Nichtschauen
Zugleich – des Menschen Trost ist Gottvertrauen.

Das Herzensauge trennt nicht Ich und Du –
Findet im Sein die Einheit und die Ruh.
Des Körpers Aug kann Gott in Bildern sehen;
Doch Sinne können nicht den Grund verstehen.

Das Unaussprechliche soll ich euch sagen?
Ein heikles Werk. Wohlan, ich will es wagen.

The Present Moment

Strange, when one compares temporality
With the mystery-land of Eternity:
What gives us the right to love the present moment?
A something eternal, from a holy Beyond.

A first thing is the happiness of possession –
A second, the nowness of experience;

A third goes back to God's very Being.

Inward Realization

Day, night; full moon, new moon, year –
Summer and winter, as it has always been.
Zenith and Nadir, North, South, East and West –
Thus is the world made, wide and strong.
Space, the wheel of time; cosmic poem –
The dance of Isis. Her face you do not see.

And then? This should not rob you of your courage –
For "blessed are they who see not, yet believe."
The wise man's gaze is both seeing and not-seeing –
Man's consolation is his trust in God.

The heart's eye does not distinguish I and thou –
It finds in Being unity and rest.
The body's eye sees God in images;
But the senses cannot grasp the essence.

Should I tell you the inexpressible?
A delicate task. But yet, I will attempt it.

Maße

Ob man sich auch um Wörter, Bilder stritte –
Die Welt ist All und Nichts. Gott ist die Mitte.

Der Kosmos dehnt sich aus, weil er erläutert
Was in der Einheit liegt. Und umgekehrt:
Er ist ein Punkt in der Allmöglichkeit –
Sie ist es, die sich grenzenlos vermehrt.

So ist es in der Seele, die sich dehnt
Ins Ungemessne, und doch wenig ist;
Das Herz ist Mitte, Kern – doch unbegrenzt;
Es ist unendlich mehr, als was man misst.

Vielheit scheint zu besiegen bloßes Eins;
Doch Einheit ist das Alles, trotz des Scheins.

Vergleiche

Ein Sonnenstern – unvorstellbare Größe;
Ich bin ein Sandkorn, das im Raum verschwindet.
Und dennoch trage ich den Stern in mir –
Er ist ein Stäubchen, das mein Geist begründet.

Denn alles Dasein ist aus Geist geboren;
Und dieses Wunder hat mir Gott geschenkt.
Gott wollte in der Welt als Zeuge leben
Und hat sein Alles in mein Nichts versenkt.

Des Menschen Sein ist mehr, als was du weißt –
Denn keinen Maßstab gibt es für den Geist.

Schönheit ist Geist – zu edler Form geronnen;
Geist hat den Stoff besiegt – für sich gewonnen.

Gewaltig scheint die Welt, die uns umgibt –

Noch größer ist, wer seinen Schöpfer liebt.

Measures

Whether one disputes over words and pictures –
The world is all and nothing. God is the Center.

The cosmos unfolds itself because it shows
What lies in Unity. Conversely,
It is a point within All-Possibility –
It is the latter which expands without bounds.

And so it is with the soul: it unfolds itself
Into the limitless, and yet is little;
The heart is center, core – yet is unbounded,
It is infinitely more than what one measures.

The many appears to overwhelm mere Oneness;
But Oneness is the All, despite appearances.

Comparisons

A sun star – unimaginably great;
I am a grain of sand that vanishes in space.
And yet I carry the star within me –
A speck of dust, and my spirit is its foundation.

For all existence is born of the Spirit,
And God has bestowed this miracle on me.
God wished to live in the world as a witness,
And so He cast His All deep into my naught.

Man's being is more than what thou knowest –
There is no measuring rod for the Spirit.

Beauty is Spirit, crystallized into noble form;
Spirit has vanquished matter, and won it for Itself.

Immense seems the world surrounding us –

Greater still is he who loves his Creator.

Ausstrahlung

Man sagt, die Erde sei zuerst gewesen;
Und dann das Leben; das Bewusstsein; dann
Der Menschengeist – das Eine aus dem Andren,
Man weiß nicht weshalb, wie und wo und wann.

In Wirklichkeit: aus unsichtbarer Mitte
Ward alles auf die Erde hingestrahlt,
Das Niedrige, das Höhere, der Geist –
So hat der Schöpfer unsre Welt gemalt.

Und alles war im Höchsten vorgezeichnet,
Ergab sich aus der Möglichkeit Gewebe.
Es ward der Mensch, auf dass ein Erdgeschöpf
Vom Höchsten zeuge und zum Himmel strebe.

Die Sanduhr

Schau auf die Sanduhr: sie ist halb gefüllt,
Und eine Hälfte leer, je nach dem Stand.
Sinnbildlichkeit: wo ist das Ja, das Nein
Im Universum – was ist Uhr und Sand?

Wenn du im Weltgetrieb die Fülle siehst,
Dann scheint dir Gott das Leere, Unsichtbare;
Doch siehst du in der Welt den hohlen Schein,
Dann weißt du: Gottes ist das Sein, das Wahre.

Der Dinge Raum ist nicht unendlich groß,
Trotz aller Vielheit Spiel; denn Gott allein
Ist die Allmöglichkeit – ist grenzenlos.

Radiation

They say that the earth came first,
Then life, consciousness, and then
Man's mind — the one out of the other,
No one knows why, how, where and when.

But in reality: out of an invisible Center
Everything was radiated onto the earth,
The lower, the higher, the spirit —
Thus did the Creator paint our world.

And all was prefigured in the Most High,
It arose from the web of Possibility.
Man came to be, so that an earthly creature
Might bear witness to God, and strive toward Heaven.

The Hourglass

Look at the hourglass: one half is full
And the other empty, depending on one's standpoint.
Its symbolism: where is the "yes" and the "no"
In the universe — what are hour and sand?

When thou seest fullness in the bustling of the world,
Then God will seem to thee as void, invisible;
But when in the world thou seest hollow show,
Then knowest thou: Being and Truth belong to God.

The space of things is not infinitely vast,
Despite the play of multiplicity; for God alone
Is All-Possibility — He alone is limitless.

Kosmosophie

Sphärenmusik – die Zahl, die Harmonie:
Pythagoras sah sie in Einem Bilde.
So ist der Geist, so ist die Welt gemacht:
Der Logik Strenge, des Gemütes Milde.

Das Denken will das Seiende umschreiben,
Und die Musik erweckt das Wunderbare.
Verstandesdenken ist wie Rechnen, Zählen;
Musik ist wie die Einfühlung ins Wahre.

Weltall

Drei Ausdehnungen hat der Raum, vier Phasen
Sind in der Zeit; dies, wenn man sie an sich
Betrachten will. Sodann hat Raum auch Mitte,
Und Zeit hat Gegenwart; darin das Ich.

Hier, Jetzt, ist Gott– unendlich, ewiglich.

Urzeichen

Der Kreis zeigt die Vollkommenheit. Und dann
Das Viereck zeigt die Welt mit ihren Türen:
Nord, Süd, Ost, West. Das Dreieck ist, was strebt:
Es will gebären; es will aufwärts führen.

Und so die Seele: sie ist reiner Geist,
Sodann Erlebniswelt: das Ich, Gefühl
Und dann die Schöpferin des guten Werks;
Und schließlich Drang zum allerhöchsten Ziel.

Cosmosophy

Music of the spheres – number and harmony:
Pythagoras saw these in one sole Image.
Thus is the Spirit, thus is the world made:
Rigor of logic and gentleness of soul.

Thought wishes to delineate what exists,
And music awakens the miraculous.
Rational thought is like reckoning or counting;
Music is like the intuition of the True.

Universe

Space has three dimensions, four phases
Are in time; so it is, when one considers them
In themselves. Then space also has a center,
And time has a present; and therein is the I.

God is Here, Now – infinite and eternal.

Primordial Signs

The circle signifies perfection. And
The square signifies the world with its doors:
North, South, East, West. The triangle is that which strives:
It wishes to give birth; it wants to lead upward.

And so too is the soul: she is pure spirit,
Then the world of experience: the I, the feelings,
Then she is the creator of good works;
And finally, the longing for the highest goal.

Urform

Für die Indianer ist das All ein Kreis;
Der Große Geist – Er liebt, bewirkt das Runde,
Weil es Vollkommenheit und Güte zeigt.

Aus Rundung ist des Weibes Leib gemacht –
Er ist das All; vom Höchsten gibt er Kunde:
Die Liebe, Wärme, die herniedersteigt.

Rund ist der Himmel, und er schenkt uns Regen –
So wirkt der Güte und der Schönheit Segen.

Auch Kindlichkeit will uns die Urform zeigen –
Rund ist das Kind, und so des Spieles Reigen.

Möge der Mensch ein schlichtes Leben führen –
Nie eine leichte Kindlichkeit verlieren.
Jedoch: die Kugel ist nicht bloß ein Kind –
Bedenkt, wie riesig Himmelskörper sind.

Guna

Sattva, Rajas und Tamas: leicht, heiß, schwer,
Könnte man sagen, je nachdem man schaut.
Er gibt in Māyā Ja, und Glut, und Nein –
Die Seel ist aus Verschiedenheit gebraut.

Doch auch im Schweren, Dunklen ist ein Gut:
Unter der Himmelsweite ruht die Erde.
Und gebe Gott, dass das, was dunkel ist
In unsrer Seel, zu Geist und Helle werde.

Primordial Form

For Indians the Universe is a circle;
The Great Spirit loves and brings forth what is round,
Because it shows perfection and goodness.

Woman's body is made of roundness –
It is the All; it bears witness to the Most High:
Love and warmth that descend to earth.

Round is the sky and it gives us rain –
Thus works the blessing of goodness and beauty.

Childlikeness too wants to shows us the primordial form –
The child is round, and so is his playful dance.

May man lead a simple life –
May he never lose a light childlikeness.
Nevertheless: the sphere is not a child only –
Think how immense celestial bodies are.

Gūna

Sattva, *rajas* and *tamas*: light, hot and heavy,
So one could say, according to one's viewpoint.
In *Māyā* there is "yes," and "heat," and "no" –
The soul is composed of variety.

But even in the heavy and dark there is a good:
The earth reposes beneath the sky's expanse.
And God grant that what is dark in our soul
May be transformed into Spirit and Light.

Das Ich

Kein Ich könnt hunderttausend Jahre dauern –
Es würd sich fühlen gleichsam hinter Mauern.
Wo ist die Heimat nach der längsten Frist?
Im Paradies, das in Gott selber ist.

Man muss verstehn: wer Ich sagt, der sagt Zeit –
Das Selbst allein ist in der Ewigkeit.
Was mag der Stoff sein, den das Schicksal knetet?
Unsterblich ist in uns der Kern, der betet.

Grenzen

Ursächlichkeitsbedürfnis: es hat Grenzen;
Verstand: er soll nicht denken, um zu glänzen.
Die Anhaltspunkte sollen ihm genügen –
Nur mit Erleuchtung kann die Seele fliegen.

Ihr sollt euch nicht mit Ungewissheit quälen –
Wer Gott hat – wen hat Gott – dem kann nichts fehlen.
Man kann gar vieles, doch nicht alles sagen;
Vertraut auf Gott – ihr sollt nicht weiter fragen.

Geschichte

Bedenke dieses: jeden Augenblick
Ist jedes Lebewesen etwas älter –
Dem Tode näher; es gibt kein Zurück.

So sind wir alle in die Weltgeschichte
Hineingewoben; alle, bis zum Letzten.
Wir stehen vor dem einen Endgerichte –

Und ist der Bauer älter, so der Kaiser.
Wir alle müssen durch den Zeitraum wandern –
Dies ist die große Frage: wer wird weiser.

The "I"

No "I" could last a hundred thousand years –
It would feel itself, so to speak, behind walls.
Where is our homeland after so long a span?
In Paradise, which is in God Himself.

One must understand: who says "I," says "time" –
The Self alone is in Eternity.
What might the substance be, that destiny kneads?
Immortal is the kernel within us that prays.

Limits

The need for causality: it has limits;
Reason: it should not think in order to dazzle.
Points of reference should suffice it –
Only with illumination can the soul fly.

You should not torment yourselves with uncertainty –
He who has God – who is God's – can lack nothing.
One can say many things, but not everything;
Trust in God – you should not ask further.

History

Reflect on this: at every instant
Each living being becomes older –
Is closer to death; there is no return.

Thus are we all woven into the world's history;
Each one of us, up to the last.
We stand before the one Last Judgment –

And if the peasant grows older, so does the emperor.
We all must journey through the space of time –
This is the great question: who becomes wiser.

Allschicksal

Das All ist wie ein einzig Lebewesen;
Ein einzig Schicksal in der Zeit, im Raum –
Zerteilt in Tausende von Einzelwesen.

Das Weltall altert, es wird langsam kälter –
So unsre Sonne; ja die größten Sterne
Wie der Antares, werden mit uns älter.

Das große Zeitrad dreht sich für und für –
Ich bin nicht einsam, alles lebt mit mir.

„Inwendig in euch ist das Himmelreich" –
Ich bin ein Funke und das All zugleich.

Grundwahrheit

Ich und die Welt: sie stehn sich gegenüber –
Doch sind sie eins – die Spaltung geht vorüber.
Ich weiß nicht, ist die ganze Welt mein Traum,
Oder bin ich von ihres Träumens Schaum.

Einbildung sei die ganze Welt, sagt einer –
Wo solches Wahnbild herkäm, das weiß keiner.
Ich oder du, wach, träumend, groß und klein –

Die Wahrheit liegt im einen, tiefen Sein.

Universal Destiny

The All is like a single living being;
A single destiny in time and space –
Divided into thousands of single beings.

The Universe is aging, it is slowly growing colder –
As is our sun; even the largest stars,
Such as Antares, grow older with us.

The great wheel of time turns on and on –
I am not alone, all things live with me.

"Within you is the Kingdom of Heaven" –
I am at once a spark and the great All.

Fundamental Truth

I and the world: they stand opposite each other –
Yet they are one – the division is impermanent.
I know not if the whole world is my dream,
Or if I am the foam of the world's dreaming.

Some say the whole world is imagination –
Whence such an illusion came, no one knows.
I or thou, awake, dreaming, great and small–

The Truth lies in the one, deep Being.

Verneinung

Dem Toren ist das Wahre einerlei:
Die Tiefenschau verkennt er; wähnt, ich sei
Bloß ein Verneiner, der die Welt zerfetzt,
Nichts gelten lässt, und siegen will zuletzt.

Versteht mich recht: Bejahung kann nicht sein
Ohne der Wahrheit wohlgewägtes Nein.

Urlicht

Siehe, das Göttliche Selbst
gibt sich kund auf verschiedene Weise —
Einmal in allen Geschöpfen,
auf allen Stufen des Daseins;
Sodann im Menschen
durch den Es als Geist sich verkündet.

Auch unterscheiden musst du:
das Edle ist nicht das Gemeine —
Unmittelbar, durch den Inhalt,
zeigt Schönheit und Adel die Selbstheit;
Mittelbar ist Sie bewiesen
durch alles, was Dasein besitzt.

Mensch, sei dir deiner bewusst:
denn das, was du bist, sollst du werden —
In deines Wesens Gewebe
zeuge vom strahlenden Selbst.

Negation

To the fool, the True is indifferent:
He misunderstands deep insight, and imagines I am
Merely a negator who tears the world apart,
Denies all values, and wants the final victory.

Understand me rightly: there can be no affirmation
Without the well-weighed "no" of Truth.

Primordial Light

Behold how the Divine Self
    reveals Itself in diverse ways —
First in all creatures,
    on all levels of existence;
Then in man,
    through whom It reveals Itself as Spirit.

Thou must also distinguish:
    The noble is not the ordinary —
Beauty and nobility manifest Selfhood
    Directly, through their content;
Indirectly, Selfhood is proven
    Through everything that has existence.

Man, be thou ever conscious of thyself:
    For what thou art, that thou shouldst become —
In the fabric of thy being
    Bear witness to the shining Self.

Wohin?

So mancher möcht auf dieser Erdenwelt
Unsterblich sein – so wie im Paradiese
Ewig im Glück auf einer Himmelswiese.
Jedoch Vergänglichkeit liegt tief im Wesen
Des Daseins selbst – Erkenntnis kann es lesen
In Dingen, im Geschehen.
Eine Frage:
Was ist im bessren Jenseits unsre Lage?
Gott wählt für uns, wir haben nichts zu wählen –
Der Mensch ist arm; dem Schöpfer kann nichts fehlen.

Des Paradieses Leben, und sein Reigen
In Seligkeit, ist auch ein Höhersteigen –
Doch jeder an dem Platz, der ihm gebührt,
Denn da ist keine Torheit, die verführt.
Im Himmelreich ist Gottes Gegenwart,
Um die ihr euch jenseits der Zeiten schart.
Auch wenn ich keine andre Antwort fände –

In Gott ist unser Ende – ohne Ende.

Whither?

So many people in this earthly world
Would like to be immortal — as in Paradise,
Eternally happy on a heavenly meadow.
But transience lies deep in the substance
Of existence itself — knowledge can read it
In things and in events.
A question:
What is our situation in the better hereafter?
God chooses for us, we have nothing to choose —
Man is poor; the Creator can lack nothing.

The life of Paradise, and its round-dance in bliss,
Is also a rising higher —
But each one in the place befitting him,
For there there is no foolishness that leads astray.
In Heaven's Kingdom is the Presence of God,
Round which ye gather, beyond all time.
Even if I could find no other answer —

In God is our end — without end.

Darshan

Ich las in einem alten Andachtsbuch:
Im Himmel zeige Jesus seine Wunden
Der Heilgen Jungfrau, dass sein Heilswerk leuchte
In ihrer Seele zu geweihten Stunden;

Maria zeige ihm dann ihren Leib,
Ihn zu erinnern, was sie ihm gegeben
Mit diesem Sakrament, von Gott bereitet:
Sein Fleisch und Blut, sein heilig Herz, sein Leben.

Darshan: die Contemplatio heilger Zeichen,
Auf dass wir ihren tiefen Sinn erreichen
Und fühlen, dass der Himmel uns belohnt –
Dass das geliebte Andre in uns wohnt.

Versteht es: zuerst Schauen, und dann Werden –
Es gibt nicht bessern Liebesblick auf Erden.

Vincit omnia

Wahrheit ist alles. Dann das weise Wollen,
Das aus dem wahren Wort wir folgern sollen.
Wär nicht die Wahrheit, gäb es keinen Geist,
Der eitler Schemen Schleier jäh zerreißt.
Wer hat euch in das Netz des Trugs getrieben?
Die Wahrheit ist in unser Herz geschrieben!

Folge dem Wahren, sei es wider Willen –
Es wird dich, Kelch, mit der Erlösung füllen.

Darshan

I read in an old prayer book:
In Heaven Jesus shows his wounds
To Mary, so that his salvation's work
Might shine, at consecrated hours, in her soul;

The Holy Virgin then shows him her body,
To remind him of what she gave him
With this sacrament, prepared by God:
His flesh and blood, his sacred heart, his life.

Darshan: the contemplation of sacred signs,
So that we may reach their deepest meaning,
And feel that Heaven is rewarding us —
That the belovèd Other dwells within.

Understand: first comes seeing, and then becoming —
There is on earth no better loving glance.

Vincit omnia

Truth is everything. Then comes the wise will
That we should draw as a consequence from the true word.
If Truth were not, there would be no mind
To rend the veil of idle schemes.
Who has driven you into illusion's net?
The Truth is written in our hearts!

Follow the True, be it against thy will —
It will fill thee, a chalice, with deliverance.

Berichtigung

Man hat gesagt: Gutes bestehe nur
Als Gegensatz zum Schlechten; wär kein Nein,
Dann wäre auch kein Ja. – Verhältnismäßig
Ist etwas dran; im Unbedingten nicht.
Denn Gut ist gut an sich, ist reines Sein –

Gäb es kein Dunkel, gäb es dennoch Licht.

Rahmah

„Meiner Barmherzigkeit Strahl –
wahrlich, er kam vor dem Zorne."
Solches sprach Gott;
und so wurde es uns überliefert.
Denn als die Welt noch nicht war,
da war nur die selige Güte.
Zorn – er war noch nicht entzündet,
er schlief in der Möglichkeit Dunkel.
Was es bedeutet?
Dies: dass der Barmherzigkeit Wärme
Tief liegt im Wesen der Gottheit –
in ihrem strahlenden Sein.

Urgesang

Sag mir, o Selbst, wo deine Schleier sind,
Die in der Welt dein Antlitz tief verhüllen
Und dennoch es enthüllen – Strahlen, die
Mit deiner Gegenwart das Weltall füllen

Und kostbar machen. Harfe der Natur,
Beglücke uns, du Urgesang der Erde,
Auf dass die Seele, aller Selbstsucht frei,
In Gottes Harmonie zur Harfe werde.

Rectification

It has been said: the good exists only
As an opposite to the bad; if there were no "no,"
There would be no "yes." – On the plane of relativity
There is something in this; but not in the Absolute.
For the Good is good in itself, it is pure Being –

Were there no darkness, there would yet be Light.

Rahmah

"The ray of My Mercy –
        verily, it came before My Wrath."
Thus spake God;
        and thus it was transmitted to us.
For when the world still was not,
        there was only blissful goodness.
Wrath – it was not yet kindled,
        it slept within the darkness of possibility.
What does this mean?
        This: that the warmth of Mercy
Lies deep in the Substance of Divinity –
        in Its radiant Being.

Primordial Song

Tell me, O Self, where are thy veils
Which in the world deeply conceal thy Face,
And yet reveal it – rays
That fill the Universe with thy Presence

And make it precious. Harp of Nature,
Bring us gladness, thou the earth's primordial song!
So that the soul, free of all self-seeking,
Become a harp within God's Harmony.

Erkennen

Hier ist Erkennen, Schau — dort bloßes Denken;
Das Herz schaut in das Wahre tief hinein —
Doch manche, sogenannte Denker, meinen
Frucht der Entwicklung müsse alles sein.

Jedoch: geschichtlich sind nur Ausdrucksweisen —
Von allem Beiwerk ist die Wahrheit rein.
Der Urgehalt liegt außerhalb der Zeiten —
Da wo der Geist ist, da sind Wirklichkeiten.

Schauendes Kennen zielt auf das, was ist —
Nicht auf des Wähnens wankendes Gerüst.
Möge die Wahrheit unser Schicksal lenken —
Uns letzten Endes die Befreiung schenken.

Skepsis

Cartesius meint: am Anfang war der Zweifel —
Mit anderm Wort: am Anfang war der Teufel,
Nämlich der Irrtum. Denn Gewissheit ist
Was überwindet allen Zweifels List.

Geistige Einfühlung, nicht Denkens Spiel
Ist Schlüssel der Erkenntnis; viel zu viel
Hat man die Zweifelsdenkerei betrieben.

Die Wahrheit steht im Herz — in Gott geschrieben.

True Knowledge

Here is true knowledge, vision – there is mere thinking;
The heart looks deep into the True –
Yet some so-called thinkers believe
That everything must be the fruit of evolution.

However: only the modes of expression are historical –
The True is free from all embellishments.
The essential Content is outside time –
Where the Spirit is, there are realities.

Visionary knowledge looks at that which is –
Not at the shaky scaffold of the imagination.
May Truth guide our destiny –
And ultimately grant us deliverance.

Skepticism

Descartes opined: in the beginning was doubt –
In other words: in the beginning was the devil,
Namely error. For certitude
Is what overcomes all the ploys of doubt.

Intellectual intuition, not the play of thought,
Is the key to Knowledge; man has engaged
Far too much in the pseudo-thinking of doubt.

Truth stands written in the heart – in God.

Sophia Perennis

Weltliche Philosophen bauen Thesen –
Ein jeder fand, was niemand fand vordem;
Ein jeder hat den Vogel abgeschossen
Mit einem neu erfundenen System.

Der Gnostiker will nur verständlich machen
Der neuen Umwelt, was man früh verstand,
Ja seit der Menschheit Ursprung – eigne Wahrheit
Ist in der Metaphysik unbekannt.

Neu können wohl Gedankengänge sein;
Der Lehre Kern ist zeitlos wie ein Stein.

West-Ost

Im Abendland heißt Mensch: der Abenteurer,
Der gerne zweifelt, alles will durchwühlen;
So braucht man eine fremde Religion
Mit Glaubenszwang, dramatischen Gefühlen;

Doch Gnosis – sie muss blühn, wo es auch sei.
So ward der Messianismus bald ein Rahmen
Der Metaphysik, griechisch oder frei –
Grundsätzlich jenseits ichbetonter Dramen.

Für Hindus ist das Heilge überall;
Für Christen beim Altar, im Glockenschall.
Wähnt nicht, der Wald sei weltlich; Heiligkeit
Ist in den Dingen, stets für Gott bereit.

Sophia Perennis

Worldly philosophers construct their theses –
Each one finds what no one found before;
Each one thinks that he has hit the mark
With a newly invented system.

The gnostic seeks only to explain
In new surroundings what always has been known,
Yea, since the origin of man – individual truth
In metaphysics is unknown.

Forms of thought may well be new;
The doctrine's kernel is as timeless as stone.

West-East

In the West, "man" means: the adventurer,
Who readily doubts and wants to probe into everything;
So he needs a religion from an outside source,
With obligatory beliefs and dramatic expressions;

But gnosis – it must bloom, wherever it may be.
And so Messianism soon became a framework
For metaphysics, whether Greek or free –
Fundamentally beyond individualistic dramas.

For Hindus, the sacred is everywhere;
For Christians, it is at the altar and in the peal of bells.
Deem not that the forest is worldly; holiness
Is in things, ever ready for God.

Das Verhältnis

Verhältnismäßig – wie die ganze Welt –
Ist das Phänomen Mensch: und unbedingt
Ist Gott allein.
                    Was zählt, ist nicht der Tand
Der Bildung, Wissenschaft, um den man ringt –

Es ist nur das Verhältnis zu dem Einen,
Das alles ist – von dem die Menschen meinen
Es sei nur Traum.
                    Wenn du an Gott dich haltest,
Ist's gleich, was du an Tätigkeit entfaltest –

Ob du an höchste Wissenschaft dich wagst
Oder den Büffel auf der Steppe jagst.

Urmensch

Des Daseins Grund: es gibt ein Urbild Mensch,
Das unbewegt in Gottes Geiste schwebt –
Ganz unberührt von allem, was der Leib,
Mit ihm die Seel, im Erdentraum erlebt.

Dies ist der Mensch: platonische Idee,
In Gottes Geist und Güte eingeschlossen –
Und dann in tausend Wesen umgegossen;
Das Leben: Frühlingsblüten, dann der Schnee –

Ein Alles und ein Nichts. All insofern,
Als wir in Gottes Weisheit sind ein Stern;
Ein Nichts, sofern wir stehen in der Welt
Vor Gott, des Macht der Dinge Sein enthält.

Urmensch: nicht bloß ausschließend ist der Sinn:
Der Einzige ist alles, was ich bin.
Sieh, wie der Dinge Rätsel sich verzweigen –

Das Wort muss sein.
                    Wahrheit durchbricht das Schweigen.

The Relationship

Relative – like the whole world –
Is the phenomenon of man: absolute
Is God alone.
                    What counts are not the trifles
Of culture and science, for which men vie –

It is only our relationship with the One
That is everything – which men think
Is but a dream.
                    If you hold fast to God,
It matters not what your pursuits may be –

Whether you venture into the highest science,
Or hunt buffalo on the prairie.

Archetypal Man

The ground of existence: there is a human archetype
That floats, motionless, within God's Spirit –
Wholly untouched by everything that the body
And with it the soul experience in the earthly dream.

This is man: a Platonic idea
Enclosed within the Spirit and Goodness of God –
And then recast into a thousand beings;
Our life: first spring blossoming, then snow –

An all and a naught. An all inasmuch
As we are a star in God's Wisdom;
A naught inasmuch as we stand in the world
Before God, whose Might contains the being of things.

Archetypal man: the meaning is not merely exclusive:
The Unique One is all that I am.
See how the enigma of things ramifies –

The Word must be.
                Truth pierces through Silence.

Richtungen

„Er ist der Erste und der Letzte; dann
Der Äußere, der Innere" – so lehrt
Der Alkorān. – Der Erste: weil Gott schafft;
Der Letzte: da die Welt zurück sich kehrt
Zum Allerhöchsten Gut, durch dessen Kraft.

Der Äußere: das Gut, das überfließt –
Gott ist die Macht, die Welt ist Widerschein.
Der Innere: Der alles Dasein misst,
Von Innen her; im Herzen wohnt das Sein.

Gott ist der Erste, weil Er Ursach ist;
Der Letzte, weil die Welt sich selbst vergisst;
Anfang und Ende –
Denn das Reich ist Dein.

Symbole

Des Heiles Wege, seine Worte –
Ihr Sinnbild sind des Raumes Orte.

Der Osten zeigt des Geistes Kraft;
Der Westen, unsrer Seele Frieden.
Der Norden strahlt die Reinheit aus;
Des Herzens Glaube glüht im Süden.

Der Himmel, mit der Bäume Kronen,
Zeiget der Wahrheit Sonnenschein;
Die Erde, wo die Wurzeln wohnen,
Ist Sinnbild für das tiefe Sein.

Gott hat in Bildern sich gedacht
Und hat daraus die Welt gemacht.

Directions

"He is the First and the Last; then
The Outward and the Inward" – so teaches the Koran.
The First: for God creates;
The Last: because the world returns
To the Sovereign Good, through the power thereof.

The Outward: the Good which overflows –
God is Power, the world is reflection.
The Inward: He Who measures all existence
From within; Being dwells in the heart.

God is the First, because He is the Cause;
He is the Last, because the world forgets itself;
Beginning and End –
for Thine is the Kingdom.

Symbols

The ways of salvation, its words –
Their symbols are the regions of space.

The East denotes the spirit's strength;
The West, our peace of soul.
The North radiates purity;
The heart's faith glows in the South.

The sky, with the tree-tops,
Shows the sunshine of Truth;
The earth, where the roots dwell,
Is a symbol for deep Being.

God conceived Himself in images,
And out of them He made the world.

Schlüssel

Sag dir, dass Gott das Jetzt ist, und verharre
In heilgem Schweigen, gottgeweihter Stille;
Ein andermal: sag dir, dass Gottes Jetzt
Die Tätigkeit betont – sei du sein Wille.

Versteh, dass Gott die Mitte ist in dir –
Verharre reglos in des Friedens Innen;
Versteh auch, dass der Herr Erbarmen ist –
Wer fest vertrauet wird das Heil gewinnen.

Und dann, ja selbst vor allem: Gott ist Eins,
Denn es gibt nicht zwei letzte Wirklichkeiten.
So sei du eins im Einen, ohne Ich –
Und mög die Gnade dich zum Selbst geleiten.

Es gibt nur Einen Pfad zum Höchsten All;
Doch mehrfach ist sein Licht – wie ein Kristall.

Keys

Tell thyself that God is the Now, and remain
In holy silence, God-consecrated stillness;
Another time, tell thyself that the Now of God
Favors activity — be thou His Will.

Understand that God is the Center within thee —
Abide motionless in the inwardness of Peace;
Understand, too, that the Lord is Mercy —
The one who firmly trusts shall gain salvation.

And then, yea, above all: God is One,
For there are not two Ultimate Realities.
So be thou one in the One, without "I" —
And may grace lead thee to the Self.

There is but one path to the Highest All;
Yet its Light is many-faceted — like a crystal.

IV

Erinnerungen

Memories

Erbschaft

„Muss irgendwo ein heilig Land
In meinem Wesen sein.
Ich stehe wie am Meeresstrand,
Blick ich in mich hinein."

Vor beinah hundert Jahren schrieb
Mein Vater diese Worte.
Das heilig Land, er fand es nicht –
Er stand vor Dschannas Pforte.

Doch nicht umsonst: die Sehnsucht trieb
Ihn in ein frommes Sterben.
Die Lieb zum Heiligen – sie blieb
In mir – in seinem Erben.

Das Paradies ist nicht so fern:
„Inwendig ist das Reich des Herrn."
Mein Vater suchte. Das war ihm
Gerechtigkeit –
Allāh karīm.

Der Lehrer

Der Lehrer Heinrich Jenny – Wegeweiser
In meiner Kindheit. Biblische Geschichte
Erzählte er mit gläubigem Gemüt –
Gott und Propheten, Wunder und Gesichte.

Einmal erzählte er wie Abraham
Einst Menschen sah, im goldnen Abendschein,
Die vor der Sonne knieten – und ich dacht:
Wie wunderbar – könnt ich ein Heide sein!

Er betete mit uns, innig und schlicht.
Mein Herz war offen – ich vergaß ihn nicht.

Heritage

"Somewhere within my being there
Must be a sacred land.
When I look inside myself
I stand as by the sea."

Almost a hundred years ago
My father wrote these words.
The sacred land he did not find –
He stood at *Janna*'s gate.

Yet not in vain: nostalgia drew
Him to a pious death.
His love toward the sacred – it
Remained in me – his heir.

For Paradise is not so far:
"God's Kingdom is within."
My father sought. And this for him
Was righteousness –
Allāh karīm.

The Teacher

The teacher Heinrich Jenny – a guide-post for me
In my childhood. He taught us Bible history
With a pious spirit – told us
About God and prophets, miracles and visions.

Once he related how Abraham
Saw men, in the golden glow of evening,
Kneeling before the sun – and I thought:
How wonderful – would that I could be a heathen!

He used to pray with us, fervently and simply.
My heart was open – I never forgot him.

Vorsehung

Es kann geschehen, dass man einem Kinde
Die Seel zerbricht – für Jahre seines Lebens –
Und dennoch bleibt sein Innerstes gesund,
Das Werk gedeiht; der Böse bellt vergebens.

Nach meines Vaters Tod wurd ich verschoben
In eine andre Welt; man wollt mich ändern;
Ich blieb mir treu und ließ die Toren toben.

Alles ist Vorsehung. Der Seele Leiden
Kann mittelbar des Geistes Wohl entfachen;
Dem auserwählten Menschen mangelt nichts –

Da Gottes Engel seinen Weg bewachen.

Sidi Achmed

Es war in Mostaghanem. Trüber Sinn
Bedrückte mich, da ich im Freien stand
Bei der Moschee. Und ein Araber kam
In schwarzem Burnuss, nahm mich bei der Hand

Und sagte mir: „Dich kenne ich seit lang;
Sprich dreimal: Führe uns den Pfad, den geraden.
Ich danke dir; auf Wiedersehn, Salām" –
Und ging. Ich war mit Segenskraft beladen.

Ich traf ihn dann in Oran. Und er sprach:
„Wenn du mit Allāh Freund wirst, bist du nie
Allein. Du hast dann alles, was du brauchst.
Man nennt mich Achmed. Hör auf mich, und sieh!"

Providence

It can happen that one breaks the soul of a child –
For years of his life – and that nonetheless
His innermost depth remains sound,
The Work thrives; the evil one barks in vain.

After my father's death I was thrust
Into another world; they wanted to change me;
But I stayed true to myself and let the fools rave.

Everything is Providence. The sufferings of the soul
Can kindle, indirectly, the well-being of the spirit;
The chosen one lacks nothing –

For God's angels keep watch over his path.

Sidi Ahmad

It was in Mostaghanem. Somber mood
Oppressed me as I stood in the open
By the mosque. And an Arab came
In black burnous, took me by the hand

And said to me: "Thee I have known for long;
Say thrice: 'Lead us on the straight path.'
I thank thee; farewell, *salām*" –
And left. I was filled with a blessèd strength.

I met him later in Oran. He said:
"If thou becomest Allāh's friend, thou wilt never be
Alone; thou wilt have all that thou needest.
They call me Ahmad. Listen to me, and see!"

El-Mu'ammar

Si Tāhir El-Mu'ammar – „der Erfüllte" –
Ein heilger Mann, des Wesen ich verehrte.
Er kam und schwieg; viel Segen war dabei –
Er war erfüllt, weil er vom Trug sich leerte.

Er war von jenen, die sich tief versenken,
In deren Schweigen man die Zeit vergisst;
Von jenen, die nicht reiche Rede schenken,
Weil ihres Wesens Strahlung alles ist.

Ain el-Qalb

Des Herzens Auge, welches Allāh sieht –
Das Ain el-Qalb – hat mir ein Scheich beschrieben:
Mit bloßem Denken kommt der Mensch nicht weit –
Wer mit dem Herzen sieht, lernt Allāh lieben.

Denn im Gehirn macht sich der Mensch Gedanken;
Im Herzen wirst du nicht an Zweifeln kranken.

Yellowtail

Die „Feder aus dem Schweif des Gelben Falken":
Er war ein Weiser aus dem Stamm der Krähen,
Sonnentanzpriester bis zu seinem Ende.
Und er war einer jener schlichten, zähen
Heiligen Männer, welche Stille lieben
Und tief verstehen, was das Sinnbild meint.
„Geheimnisperlen", seine Gattin, war
Ein starker, guter Mensch. Sie sind nun drüben –
Der Tod hat sie im Großen Geist vereint.

Er war ein Mann, der inniglich versteht
Auf was es ankommt: dauerndes Gebet.

Al-Mu'ammar

Sidi Tāhir Al-Mu'ammar – "the Fulfilled" –
A holy man whose being I revered.
He came and he was silent; there was much blessing –
He was fulfilled, because he had emptied himself of illusion.

He was one of those who are deeply absorbed,
And in whose silence one forgets all time;
One of those who do not give long speeches,
Because their being's radiance is everything.

'Ayn al-Qalb

The heart's eye, which sees Allāh –
The *'Ayn al-Qalb* – a shaykh described to me:
With mere thinking, one does not go far –
Who sees with the heart, learns to love Allāh.

For in the brain man produces thoughts;
But in the heart thou wilt not be ill from doubt.

Yellowtail

"Tail feather of the Yellow Hawk":
He was a wise man of the Crow tribe,
And Sun Dance priest until his end.
He was one of those simple, tough
Holy men, who love silence
And deeply understand what symbols mean.
"Medicine Beads," his wife, was a strong,
Good person. Now they are both on the other side –
Death has united them in the Great Spirit.

He was a man who intimately understood
What counts most: perpetual prayer.

Red Cloud

Er war der Enkelsohn von „Rote Wolke“
Vom Stamm der Ogalalla. Und wir hatten
Ein lang Gespräch, der edle Greis und ich –
In Pine-Ridge, unter eines Baumes Schatten.

Er sprach zuerst von alten Zeiten; dann
War Schweigen, bis von andrem ich begann
Zu reden: dass die Welt ein Traumstoff sei –
Das Träumen geht am Wirklichen vorbei.

In seinen Stamm nahm mich der Häuptling auf,
Gab mir manch gutes Wort, und starb darauf.
Lass übers weite Land die Winde wehen –
Beim Großen Geiste wird das Herz bestehen.

Tshante-Ishta

Den Seher der Lakota, „Schwarzer Hirsch“,
Hörte ein Freund des Herzens Aug erwähnen –
Das Tshante-Ishta – das das Wahre schaut.

Wohl dem, der nicht nur seinen Sinnen traut –
Des Herzens Blick stillt unser tiefstes Sehnen.

Dies hatte auch der „Schwarzer Hirsch“ gesagt:
Die Welt – ein Traum, in dem man Schatten jagt.
Vorbei geht alles, was der Mensch erzählt –
Im Unsichtbaren ist die wahre Welt.

Red Cloud

He was the grandson of Red Cloud
Of the Oglala band. We had
A long talk, the noble old man and I –
In Pine Ridge, beneath the shade of a tree.

He talked first about old times; then there was
Silence, until I began to speak, saying:
The word is a dream-stuff –
The dream vanishes before Reality.

The Chief adopted me into his tribe,
Gave me many good words, and later died.
Let the winds sweep over the wide land –
The heart will live forever in the Great Spirit.

Chante Ishta

A friend heard Black Elk, the visionary
Of the Lakota, mention the eye of the heart –
The *Chante Ishta* – which sees the True.

Blessèd is he who does not trust his senses alone –
The vision of the heart stills our deepest longing.

This also Black Elk has said:
The world – a dream, where one chases after shadows.
All that men tell of passes away –
In the Invisible is the true world.

Der Jagadguru

Ich hab ihn nie gesehen. Doch wir grüßten
Uns durch die Freunde, die nach Indien reisten;
Mein Werk war ihm bekannt; ich kannte ihn
Durch Hindus, die ihn ehrfurchtsvoll umkreisten.

Erbe des großen Shánkara, war er
Der weise Träger der Vedānta-Leuchte;
Ein Gottesmann, der freundlich mein gedacht —
Den meines Herzens Gruß von fern erreichte.

Ramdas

Ramdas mit seinen Jüngern kam:
Sie sangen „Jai Ram Jai Jai Ram."
Es tönte wie des Ganges Wogen —
So kamen sie dahergezogen.

Ein heilger Abend — bis zur Nacht
Mit ihm und seinem Kreis verbracht;
Wir konnten geistig uns beschenken —
Wir waren eins im Gottgedenken.

Indien

Die Luft war schwer, gefüllt mit Geisteszauber —
Es war das alte Indien, reich an Farben;
Halbnackte Männer, Frauen, nackte Kinder;
Sādhus, die sich des Karma Gunst erwarben
Durch Mantras, die sie murmelten im Gehen.

Ein Tempel: ein paar schöne Frauen stehen
In goldnen Saris auf der Treppe Stufen;
Die Vina singt. Glutheiße Winde wehen —
Und aus der Ferne hört man Pfauen rufen.

The Jagadguru

I never saw him. But we greeted
Each other through friends who traveled to India;
He knew of my work; I knew him
Through Hindus who reverently surrounded him.

Heir of the great Shankara, he was
The wise bearer of the Vedanta-light;
A man of God, who thought of me kindly –
The greeting of my heart reached him from afar.

Ramdas

Ramdas came with his disciples:
They were singing: "*Jai Ram, Jai Jai Ram.*"
It sounded like the Ganges' waves –
This was how they came wandering.

A holy evening – and into the night,
We spent with him and his circle.
We could give to each other spiritually –
We were one in God-remembrance.

India

The air was heavy, filled with the Spirit's magic –
Here was old India, rich in colors;
Half-naked men and women, naked children;
Sādhus, who were earning karma's favor
Through mantras, which they murmured as they went.

A temple: a few beautiful women
Stand in golden saris on its steps;
The *vina* sings. Oppressively hot winds blow –
And far away one hears the peacocks call.

Mittelmeer

Gott und das Herz sind Mitte. Doch die Welt
Ist was uns außen in die Augen fällt –
Erinnerungen, die wir mit uns tragen;
Von schönen Orten möchte ich euch sagen.

Die Stadt Venedig, blühend auf dem Meere,
Siena, Florenz, gebührt Erinnrungs Ehre.
San Marco hält die Seel in goldnem Bann –
Und Dantes Stadt, wo er sein Werk begann.

Dann Andalusien: Córdoba, Sevilla –
Madonnenprozessionen, Laute, Tanz.
Sodann Marokko: Fes und Marrakesch –
Gebetswelt in der Spätzeit Abendglanz.

Ganz andre Welt der Griechen: auf dem Lande
Fühlst du des alten Hellas freie Helle;
Und dann, in goldbeladnen Heiligtümern,
Byzantions Weihrauch an des Himmels Schwelle.

Hier Delphi und Eleusis; Kaisariani
Und Mistra dort. Altes Mysterienland –
Pythagoras und Plato; dann Berg Athos –
Mystischer Kelch, gefüllt bis an den Rand.

Heimatklänge

Waldsee, dann Rothenburg und Dinkelsbühl;
Altstädte, die an ferne Heimat mahnen –
An Märchenbücher, seelenvolle Lieder;
In alten Gassen lebt die Seel der Ahnen.

Wo ist die Heimat? Wo ich Gott erlebte –
Da wo mein Herz in seinem Licht erbebte.

The Mediterranean

God and the heart are center. But the world
Is what outwardly strikes our eye —
Memories, that we carry with us;
Of beautiful places I would like to tell.

The city of Venice, blooming on the sea,
Siena and Florence, merit the honor of remembrance.
San Marco holds the soul in a golden spell —
And Dante's city, where he began his work.

Then Andalucía: Córdoba, Sevilla —
Madonna processions, lute and dance.
And then Morocco: Fez and Marrakesh —
A world of prayer in the evening-glow of latter times

Quite another world is Greece:
In the country you feel the free clarity of ancient Hellas,
And then, in gold-laden sanctuaries,
Byzantium's incense at the threshold of Heaven.

Here Delphi and Eleusis; there Kaisariani
And Mistra. Ancient land of mysteries —
Pythagoras and Plato; then Mount Athos —
Mystical chalice, filled up to the brim

Sounds of the Homeland

Waldsee, then Rothenburg and Dinkelsbühl;
Old towns that bring to mind a distant home —
Books of fairy-tales, soulful songs;
The souls of ancestors live in those old streets —

Where is my home? Where I experienced God —
Where my heart vibrated in His Light.

Begegnungen

Nicht Menschen nur, auch manche Erdendinge
Können bedeutende Begegnung sein;
So war in meiner Kindheit Märchentagen
Ein Freund der dunkelgrüne Rhein.

Später: der große See beim Alpenland,
Wo ich so manches Jahr gewohnt –
Er hat mit seiner Fläche Seligkeit
Mein vielgeplagtes Herz belohnt.

Das Wallis mit den schneebedeckten Bergen,
Die zeitlos in den Himmel ragen;
Das königliche Matterhorn – die Täler,
Die Teppiche von Blumen tragen.

Und dann der wilde Wald im fernen Westen,
Einst der Indianer heilig Land.
Das Frühste und das Späteste im Leben
Sind nah – sie reichen sich die Hand.

Intermezzo

Es mag sich so ergeben: man darf wählen
Ob man belehren soll, oder erzählen.

Denn es ist wahr – und Wahres hat zu gelten:
Wir leben in zwei Seelen, in zwei Welten.

An Gutem, Schönem, darf der Mensch sich freuen –
Gott fordert nicht, dass wir nicht Menschen seien.

Encounters

Not only people, but also earthly things
Can be a meaningful encounter;
Thus, in my childhood's fairy-tale days,
The dark green Rhine was a friend.

Later: the big lake near the Alps
Where I lived for so many years –
With the blissfulness of its surface,
It recompensed my much-tormented heart.

Then Valais with its snowcapped mountains,
Which tower timelessly into the sky;
The kingly Matterhorn – the valleys,
Wearing carpets of wild flowers.

Then the wild forests in the Far West,
Once the Indian's sacred land.
The earliest and latest in one's life
Are near – they take each other's hand.

Intermezzo

It can happen that one has the right to choose
Whether one ought to instruct, or to recount.

For it is true – and the true has to assert itself:
We live in two souls, in two worlds.

Man has the right to delight in the good and the beautiful –
God does not demand that we not be men.

Westwärts

Indianer reiten; unvergesslich Bild –
Der eine nach dem andern, stolz zu Pferde,
Mit Federschmuck an Haupt und Lanze; wild
Und groß – Kriegsgötter, doch von dieser Erde.

Lebensweg

Zuerst die Stadt – zuletzt der freie Wald;
Dies ist mein Weg durchs Leben, möcht ich sagen.
Die Stadt – sie bietet manche traute Freud;
Ich wollt den Traum nicht bis zum Ende tragen.

Der Wald ist Urwelt; Gottes Duft ist nah.
Kein Lärm der Leute; Laute der Natur.
Dies ist die Außenwelt – denn innerlich
Ist Gottes Reich, und seine Gnade nur.

Das Heim

Bergiger Wald. In seiner tiefen Mitte
Ein klarer Bach; oben das hölzern Haus
Mit der Veranda, die sich westwärts windet
Und meine Wohnung mit dem Wald verbindet.

Und eine wilde Wiese um das Haus;
Und ein Indianerzelt, auch hohe Fichten;
Ein Blumenteppich; Hirsche kommen her.
Ich könnte mir kein bessres Heim erdichten

Auf dieser Erde und im Reich der Zeit.
Mein zeitlos Herz wohnt in der Ewigkeit.

Westward

Indians riding; an unforgettable picture –
The one after the other, proudly mounted,
With feather ornaments on head and lance;
Wild and great – war gods, yet of this earth.

Life's Path

First the city – last the free forest;
This was my path through life, so I might say.
The city offered many a familiar joy;
But I did not wish to carry this dream to the end.

The forest is primordial world; God's perfume is near.
No noise of people, only sounds of nature.
This is the outer world – for inwardly
Is God's Kingdom, and His Grace alone.

Home

Rolling forest. In its deep center,
A clear brook; above, the wooden house
With the veranda, that winds westward
And links my abode with the trees.

A wild meadow around my house;
An Indian tent, some tall pines too;
A carpet of flowers; the deer come here.
I could not imagine a better home

Upon this earth, and in the realm of time.
My timeless heart dwells in Eternity.

Tanzīh, Tashbīh

Tanzīh, das Schaun der ewigen Gesetze
Abseits der Welt, jenseits von Sinnendingen;
Tashbīh – in Sufi-Sprache – das Durchschauen,
Wie Gottes Strahlen schöne Form durchdringen.

Gott ist in nichts, und doch ist Er in allem
Was von Ihm zeugen kann; in edlen Frauen,
In edler Kunst und Wundern der Natur –

In deiner Tiefe eint sich beides Schauen.

Leitgedanken

Willst du nicht deines Lebens Sinn verlieren,
Müssen dich Leitgedanken zielwärts führen.
Gewissheit kam vom Himmel her zur Erde,
Auf dass des Daseins Sinn erfüllet werde.

Gewiss ist, dass vor Gott die Seele schweigt;
Und dann: dass Gottgedenken beste Tat;
Und dass in Gott ich finde meine Ruh;
Dass, wer Ihn gläubig ruft, Erlösung hat.
Gewiss ist: Wirklichkeit ist Er allein;
Im Gottgedenken ist mein wahres Sein.

Ein Ende hat die Lehr, wie alles Sinnen –
Doch jedes Ende ist ein neu Beginnen.

Tanzīh, Tashbīh

Tanzīh, the vision of eternal laws
Apart from the world, beyond the things of the senses;
Tashbīh – in Sufi language – the penetrating vision,
How God's Rays shine through a beautiful form.

God is in nothing, yet He is in everything
That can bear witness to Him: in noble women,
In noble art and miracles of nature –

Within thy depth both visions become one.

Guiding Themes

If thou wilt not lose the meaning of thy life,
Then guiding themes must lead thee to the goal.
Certainty came from Heaven down to earth,
That the meaning of existence might be fulfilled.

Certain it is, that before God the soul is silent;
And then, that God-remembrance is the best of acts;
And that in God I find my rest;
That whoever calls on Him with faith, has salvation.
It is certain: He alone is Reality;
And in God-remembrance is my true being.

The doctrine has an end, like all thinking –
But each end is a new beginning.

Halt ein

Des Lebens Strom – er will uns mit sich ziehen,
Will nicht, dass vor dem Sein wir stehen bleiben;
Er möchte uns in eitles Blendwerk treiben –
So dass wir unterwegs vergehn, verblühen.

Der Fromme und der Weise stehen still
Im Lebensstrome, denn die Zeit hat Stunden,
Die Gott gehören.
                Lass das Herz erkunden
Was Wahrheit ist, und was der Wahre will.

Lehrgedichte

Die Lehrgedichte – siehe, sie verbinden
Die Metaphysik mit Musik; sie dringen
Ins Innere, ohn allzuviele Mühe,
Um Seel und Herz zum Höchsten zu beschwingen.

Dem Sänger gab der Himmel edles Wort,
Den Liederkranz aufs Beste abzuschließen;
Denn alles muss zu einem Ende kommen –
So auch der Dichtung unermüdlich Fließen.

Non dignus – schwach ist alle Erdenkunst.
Der Dichter mag uns seine Gabe gönnen:
Doch weder Wahrheit, noch der Schönheit Schatz
Kann sich erschöpfen durch des Menschen Können.
Kein Menschenwort kann Gottes Wunder zeigen –

Vor seinem ewgen Worte lasst uns schweigen.

Pause

Life's river – it wants to pull us with it,
And does not want us to stand still before Being;
It would like to drive us into vain deception –
So that on the way we fade and disappear.

The pious and the wise stand still
In the river of life, for time has hours
That belong to God.
Let the heart discover
What Truth is, and what the True wills.

Didactic Poems

Didactic poems – see how they combine
Metaphysics with music; they penetrate
Inward without too much effort,
To uplift our soul and heart to the Most High.

Heaven gave the singer a noble word,
That he might best close this garland of songs;
For all things must come to an end –
And so too poetry's untiring flow.

Non dignus – feeble is all earthly art.
The poet may favor us with his gift:
Yet neither Truth, nor Beauty's treasure
Can be exhausted by human ability.
No human word can show God's wonders –

Before His eternal Word let us be silent.

Der Ring

Die Geistesbotschaft ist ein Zauberring:
Sie hatte keinen Anfang, hat kein Ende.
Wo ihr Dein Denken auch begegnen mag:
Es ist, als ob es nichts und alles fände.

Des Geistes Botschaft ist ein Zauberkreis,
Von dessen Hin und Her der Mensch nichts weiß.
„Hörst du den Wind? Er wehet, wo er will" —
Doch in des Herzens Tiefe steht er still.

Alles in Einem, Eins in Allem strahlt
In jedem Punkte, den die Kreisung malt.

Manuscript page in the author's hand

Der Ring

The Ring

I

Lehre

Doctrine

Der Ring

Die Geistesbotschaft ist ein Zauberring:
Sie hatte keinen Anfang, hat kein Ende.
Wo ihr dein Denken auch begegnen mag:
Es ist, als ob es nichts und alles fände.

Des Geistes Botschaft ist ein Zauberkreis,
Von dessen Hin und Her der Mensch nichts weiß.
„Hörst du den Wind? Er wehet, wo er will" –
Doch in des Herzens Tiefe steht er still.

Alles in Einem, Eins in Allem strahlt –
In Jedem Punkte, den die Kreisung malt.

Vom Selbst

So wie die Funken aus dem Feuer sprühen,
Oder wie Tropfen eines Wasserfalls –
So hat das Selbst sich scheinbar aufgeteilt:
Die Seelen in der Spielerei des Alls.

So ward das Selbst vieltausendmal ein Andrer –
Es ward sich fremd, tief in die Welt verirrt.
Die Wahrheit strahlt – möge die Seel sie finden,
Erleben, bis sie ganz sich selber wird!

Der Geist – er hat sich mit dem Stoff vermischt,
So das Bewusstsein seiner selbst verwischt –
Dies war ein Schicksal, das der Höchste schuf:

Befreit zu werden durch der Wahrheit Ruf.

The Ring

The Spirit's message is a magic ring:
It had no beginning, it has no end.
Wherever thy thinking may encounter it:
It is as if it found nothing and everything.

The Spirit's message is a magic circle,
Of whose coming and going man knows not.
"Hear'st thou the wind? It bloweth where it listeth" –
Yet in the depth of the heart it stands still.

Everything shines in One, One shines in everything –
In every point along the circle's turning.

On the Self

Like sparks that spray out of the fire,
Or like drops of a waterfall,
So has the Self seemingly divided Itself
Into the souls of the Universe's play.

The Self became an "other" many thousand times –
Became a stranger to Itself, lost deep in the world.
But Truth shines – and may the soul find
And experience It, until it becomes wholly itself!

The Spirit mixed Itself with matter,
And consciousness of Itself was blurred –
This was a destiny, created by the Most High:

To be set free by the call of the True.

Verwechslung

Man hat gesagt, der Mensch sei Einbildung –
Es sei das Selbst, das durch die Leiber geht.
Ein Spiel mit Worten; es ist nicht das Selbst,
Was ihr auf dieser Erde gehen seht.

Ohne die Selbstheit wär die Ichheit nicht –
Und dies genügt. Die Selbstheit lebt im Ich,
Von fern und tief, doch sie allein ist wahr.
Was wollt ihr mehr? Seid nicht so wunderlich.

Dialektik hat uns manchen Sinn verdreht –
Seid froh, dass das, was ist, geschrieben steht.

Raum-Zeit

Unendlich ist der Raum, die Zeit –
    Wir können's nicht erfassen.
Wir müssen uns in ihrem Bann
    Durchs Leben tragen lassen.
Wir wissen nicht, was beide sind –
    Nur, dass sie Gott beweisen.
Denn da sie da sind, ist gewiss,
    Dass sie den Herrn umkreisen.
O Wunder, dass es in der Welt
    Bewusstsein gibt und Minne –
Dass in des Alls Unendlichkeit
    Ein Herz das Heil gewinne.

Confusion

It has been said that man is an illusion –
That it is the Self which journeys through bodies.
A play with words; it is not the Self
That you see walking on this earth.

Without Selfhood, "I-hood" would not exist –
And this suffices. Selfhood lives in the I,
From afar and deeply, yet It alone is true.
What more do you want? Do not wonder so.

Dialectics has distorted some of our thinking –
Be glad that that which is, is written.

Space-Time

Space and time are infinite –
We cannot fathom them.
Throughout life, we must let ourselves
Be drawn into their spell.
We do not know what either is –
Only that they prove God.
For it is certain, since they exist,
They circle round the Lord.
O wonder, that in the world there are
Both consciousness and love –
That in the All's infinity
A heart may win salvation.

Fortsetzung

Da ist die Form, und neben ihr die Zahl –
Das Festgeronnene, das Fortbewegte.
Da ist die Eigenart, die Vielheit dann,
Die Gott zur Möglichkeit des Einen legte.

Die Form ist Sein. Was ist der Sinn der Zahlen?
Des Daseinswunders unbegrenztes Strahlen.
Und von des Kosmos Mächten, die wir kennen,
Sind auch Materie, Energie zu nennen:
Hier wieder Sein und Strahl: der Stoff, die Kraft,
Deren Zusammenspiel das Weltall schafft.

Das All

Das All ist einerseits ein Kreis mit Kreisen
Und andrerseits ein Strahlen wie von Sternen;
Ursprung der Dinge kann nicht sein am Rand
Wie heut die Kinder es in Schulen lernen.

Die Schöpfung kommt von Innen, nie vom Kreise;
Was auf dem Kreis geschieht, ist Nachhall nur.
Gott ist der Kern, die Mitte; lehret nicht
Natur sei Gott, und Gott sei die Natur.

Sein ist Gesetz. Die Welt – Mathematik;
Doch nicht nur dies. Das Weltall ist Musik.

Continuation

There is form, and beside it number –
Crystallization, and movement.
There is the unique, then the multiple
Which God added to the possibility of the one.

Form is being. What is the meaning of number?
The limitless radiation of the miracle of existence.
And amongst the cosmic powers known to us,
Matter and energy are also to be named:
Here again are being and radiation: substance and power,
Whose interplay creates the Universe.

The Universe

On the one hand the Universe is a circle with circles,
And on the other hand, a radiation like that of a star;
The origin of things cannot be on the periphery,
As children learn today in school.

Creation comes from the inside, never from the circle;
What happens on the circumference is merely an echo.
God is the kernel, the center; do not teach
That nature is God and God is nature.

Being is law. The world – mathematics;
Yet not this alone. The Universe is music.

Ausgangspunkt

Brahma Satyam, jagan mithyā:
Wahr ist Brahma, Welt ist Schein;
Satyān nāsti paro dharmah:
Wahrheit ist der Pflichten Sein.

Wahrheitskenntnis bringt das Müssen;
Rechtes Tun ist wahres Wissen.

Realitas

Wirklichkeit: das Große Eine.
Einerseits: Es ist An-Sich;
Andrerseits: Es ist das reine
An-Sich-Sein als Gottes Ich.

Wahlspruch

Keine Gottheit, nur die Eine:
Lā ilāha illa 'Llāh.
Alles ist in Gottes Händen:
Kullu shay'in 'inda 'Llāh.

Bessres kann der Geist nicht sagen;
Und das Herz darf nicht verzagen.

Sapientia

Die Einzigkeit des Wahren ist Erkennen
Im Raum des Denkens. Einung mit dem Wahren
Im Raum des Herzens ist die andre Seite
Der Weisheit. Gott will beides offenbaren.

Starting-point

Brahma Satyam, jagan mithyā:
Brahma is true, the world is appearance;
Satyān nāsti paro dharmah:
Truth is the essence of our duties.

Knowledge of Truth brings obligations;
Right doing is true knowing.

Realitas

Reality: the Great One.
On the one hand: It is In-Itself;
On the other hand: It is pure
In-Itself-hood as God's "I."

Maxim

No God but the One alone:
Lā ilāha illā 'Llāh.
All lies in the Hands of God:
Kullu shay'in 'inda 'Llāh.

The mind can say no better thing;
And the heart should not despond.

Sapientia

The unicity of the True is knowledge
In the space of thought. Union with the True
In the space of the heart is the other side of wisdom.
God wishes to manifest both.

Zweiklang

Das Unbedingte – das Gewaltige
Das alle Größe, alle Macht enthält;
Das Heilige – die Andacht und die Liebe –
Das wie ein Segen in die Seele fällt.

Weisheit und Heiligkeit – sie sind die Triebe
Des Herrn: schöpfend, erlösend unsre Welt.

In anderen Worten

Ursein, Sein, Dasein – Wurzel, Krone, Zweige;
Ursein ist unpersönlich, Sein persönlich,
Und Dasein vielpersönlich. Ursein ist
Unendlich fern; Sein ist nah, ist versöhnlich.

Und Dasein ist das, was wir sind: zerspalten
In abertausend Wesen, die sich lieben
Und hassen. Manche hier, und mehr noch drüben,
Bei Gott – erneute, himmlische Gestalten.

Ursein: Allmöglichkeit; Sein: Schöpferkraft;
Dasein: die Schöpfung, die das Leben schafft.

Double Harmony

The Absolute – the Mighty,
Which contains all greatness and all power;
The Holy – devotion and love –
Which descends into the soul like a blessing.

Wisdom and holiness – they are the driving forces
Of the Lord, creating and delivering our world.

In Other Words

Beyond-Being, Being, Existence – root, crown, branches;
Beyond-Being is non-personal, Being is personal,
Existence, multi-personal. Beyond-Being is
Infinitely far; Being is close, reconciling.

And Existence is that which we are: split
Into thousands upon thousands of beings who love
And hate each other. Some here, and many more hereafter
With God – renewed, heavenly beings.

Beyond-Being: All-Possibility; Being: Creative Power;
Existence: Creation, which gives rise to life.

II

Bilder

Images

Fern-Ost

Man spricht vom Griechenwunder; zweifelhaft
Ist die Erscheinung – ein zweischneidig Schwert.
Eindeutig ist das Wunder Japans, das
Zum Größten in der Künste Welt gehört.

Denn Japans Kunst verbindet Reichtum, Pracht
Mit Einfachheit – des Shintō Geistesmacht;
Und wie ein Mythos ist des Schönen Sieg,
Der mit der Sonne aus dem Meere stieg.

Rollbilder

Die grauen Tuschgemälde der Chinesen:
Berg, Bach und Wald, die aus dem Nebel steigen –
Als wollt der Erde Schönheit, wie im Traume
Den Schleier lüftend, ihre Tiefe zeigen –

Die Tiefe, die Yin-Yang und Tao birgt –
Wie Himmelsbalsam auf die Seele wirkt.

Plato

Klassische Kunst: gefühlsbetont, doch kalt –
Nachahmung der Natur, ihr dennoch feind.
Für Plato war Ägyptens Kunst der Halt
Des Schönen: das mit Wahrem sich vereint.

Far-East

One speaks of the Greek miracle; it is
A dubious phenomenon — a two-edged sword.
But unambiguous is the Japanese miracle,
Which belongs to the greatest in the world of arts.

For Japan's art combines richness and splendor
With simplicity — the spiritual power of Shintō;
And the victory of Beauty, like an ancient myth,
Rises, with the sun, out of the sea.

Scrolls

The gray ink paintings of the Chinese:
Mountain, stream and forest, emerging from the mist —
As if earth's beauty, lifting her veil
As in a dream, wished to show her depth —

The depth that contains Yin-Yang and the Tao —
Acts on the soul like Heaven's balm.

Plato

Classical art: sentimental, but cold —
Imitating nature, yet alien to it.
For Plato, Egypt's art was the support
Of the Beautiful: the beautiful that unites itself with the True.

Miniaturen

Die Hindu-Malerei will ich erwähnen
Mit ihren kindlich-märchenhaften Szenen;
Krishna und Rādhā, Flötenspiel und Reigen –
Die Blumen, die sich vor der Sonne neigen.

All dies ist Līlā, Māyās Spiel und Glück –
Des Daseins Urgewebe ist Musik.
Gewiss, da sind auch Drachen und Dämonen –

Und nackte Sādhus, die in Brahma wohnen.

Andalucia

Granada, Córdoba, Sevilla und
Manch andre Stadt – ich kenne eure Straßen
Und Innenhöfe, die der Jungfrau sind –
Doch Maghrebs Pracht und Seele nicht vergaßen.

Cantar, bailar

Südspanische Musik – sie will erklingen
Bei den Corridas, bei Zigeunertänzen;
Dann die Saetas, wenn Marienbilder
Im Scheine hoher Andachtskerzen glänzen –
Maurische Laute, deren Zauberklang
Von Tanz und Kampf zur Macarena drang.

Alt-Andalusien – farbenreiche Plätze,
Wo Weltliches und Heilges sich begegnen;
Madonnenbilder, die die Nächte segnen –
Im stillen Beten sind die tiefsten Schätze.

Miniatures

I wish to mention Hindu paintings,
With their child-like fairy-tale scenes;
Krishna and Rādhā, flute-play and circling dance –
Flowers that bow before the sun.

All this is *Līlā*, *Māyā*'s play and happiness –
The primordial fabric of Existence is music.
Of course, there are also dragons and demons –

And naked *sādhus*, who dwell in Brahma.

Andalucía

Granada, Córdoba, Sevilla
And many other cities – I have known your streets
And courtyards, which are dedicated to the Virgin –
Yet have not forgotten the soul and splendor of the Maghrib.

Cantar, bailar

Music of Southern Spain – it loves to resound
At bull fights and at gypsy dances;
Then the *saetas*, when statues of Mary
Gleam in the light of tall altar candles –
Moorish lute, whose magic sound
Of dance and battle reaches the Macarena.

Old Andalusia – colorful squares
Where the worldly and the holy meet;
Images of the Virgin that bless the nights –
In silent prayer lie the deepest treasures.

Fächerspiel

Ist nicht die Welt – an sich und in uns selbst –
Ein offner Fächer, der sich schließen kann?
Sei es, dass Gott der Welt ein Ende setzt –
Sei es, dass sich der Mensch auf Gott besann.

Kásaki

Ich hörte mehrmals singende Kosaken –
Mit tiefen, starken Stimmen. Stets zu Pferde
In ihrer Heimat – Ostaritzas Erben,
Beherrschten sie die angestammte Erde.

Reiten – am Don, am Kuban. Kampf, Gesang,
Stets vorwärts drängend, stets bereit zu sterben –
Ein wilder, lyrischer Zusammenklang.
Der Skamarinski-Tanz, die Balalaika –

Der Gnadenjungfrau Bild – Wladimirskaja.

Wanderschaft

Vom Russenpilger habt ihr wohl gehört:
Mit dem Gebet im Herz, mit einem Buch –
Philokalie – wollt er ins Weite wandern
Von einem gottgeweihten Ort zum andern,
Unter der Jungfrau gnadenreichen Stern,
Teils bittend, teils vertrauend; Preis dem Herrn!

Mit Offenbarungsbuch und Herzenswort,
Und allen eitlen Erdenwünschen fern –
Gott ist der frommen Wandrung letzter Ort.

Play of the Fan

Is not the world — both in itself and in ourselves —
An open fan that can be closed?
Be it because God brings the world to an end —
Or because man has remembered God.

Kásaki

I have several times heard Cossacks singing —
With deep, strong voices. Ever on horseback
In their homeland — heirs of Ostaritza,
They ruled over ancestral lands.

Riding — by the Don and the Kuban. Combat, song,
Ever pressing forward, ever ready to die —
A wild and lyrical harmony.
The Skamarinski-dance, the balalaika —

The image of our Lady of Mercy — Vladimirskaya.

Wandering

You have doubtless heard of the Russian pilgrim:
With prayer in his heart and with a book —
The *Philokalia* — he wished to wander far and wide
From one God-consecrated place to another,
Under the Virgin's star of grace,
Partly begging, partly trusting; praise the Lord!

With Revelation's book and the Word of the heart,
And far from all vain worldly desires —
God is the final place of this pious wandering.

Rheinland

Kindheit am Rhein. Uraltes Märchenland –
Heimat der Lieder und der Heldensagen.
Das Traumerlebnis einer Kinderseele;
Ihr unbewusstes Schauen wollte fragen:
Wo gehst du hin, o Strom, wo kommst du her?

Der Mythos von der Quelle und vom Meer:
Die Quelle, die das junge Ich verkündet;
Das Meer – das Selbst – in dem die Form verschwindet.

Lac Léman

Der Genfersee – hier wohnt ich vierzig Jahre.
Der See, im Hintergrund die Bergeshöhen;
Der Weg den See entlang; Vergangenheit.
Die Welt entschwindet, wie die Winde wehen.

Ein Traumgewebe ist des Lebens Kleid –
Das Herz – in Gott – lebt außerhalb der Zeit.

Midwest

Der Mittelwesten: maisbebaute Felder,
Kleinere Städte – und dann Wälder, Wälder;
Anfang der Wildnis und Indianerbrüder –
Landschaft des Friedens und der letzten Lieder.

Rhineland

Childhood by the Rhine. Fairy-tale land of old –
Home of songs and heroic sagas.
The dream-experience of a child's soul;
Its unconscious gaze wanted to ask:
Whither goest thou, O river, and whence dost thou come?

Myth of the source and of the sea:
The source, which proclaims the young I;
The sea – the Self – in which form disappears.

Lac Léman

Lake Geneva – here I lived for forty years.
The lake, in the background the mountain peaks;
The path along the lake – all this is of the past.
The world fades away, as blow the winds.

Life's garment is a web of dreams –
The heart – in God – lives ever outside time.

Midwest

The Midwest: fields planted with corn,
Little towns – then forests, forests;
Beginning of the wilderness and Indian brethren –
Landscape of peace and of last songs.

III

Mitteilungen

Messages

Sprachen

Jedwelche Sprache ist wie eine Seele,
Sagt Aristoteles. Eine von ihnen
Ist unser Seelengrund; die andern sind
Wie Sonnenstrahlen, die ins Innre schienen.

Und jede Sprache hat ihr eignes Gutes:
Da ist das strenge, sachliche Latein;
Da ist das bildervolle, tiefe Deutsch;
Man möcht etwas von jeder Sprache sein.

Und da sind Sprachen, die der Herr geredet,
Uns zu erleuchten auf verschiedne Weise;
Laut spricht der Herr in jeder Heilgen Schrift –
In Herzens heilger Kammer spricht Er leise.

Schreiben

Handschrift ist wesentlich. Der Grundsatz ist:
Ein jedes Zeichen muss erkennbar sein;
Man darf sie nicht verwechseln. Wenn dies stimmt,
Dann unterscheide zwischen Mein und Dein.

Nach eitler Eigenart soll niemand trachten;
Nur auf den innern Adel darfst du achten.

Languages

Each language is like a soul,
Said Aristotle. One of them is
Our own soul's ground; the others are
Like sun-rays that shine into us.

And each language has its own virtue:
There is Latin, objective and severe;
There is German, imaginative and profound;
Something of each language one would like to be.

And there are the languages that the Lord has spoken,
To enlighten us in different ways;
God speaks aloud in every sacred Scripture –
In the holy chamber of the heart, He speaks softly.

Writing

Handwriting is important. Its principle is:
Each sign must be identifiable;
They should not be confused. Once this is in order,
Then distinguish between mine and thine.

No one should endeavor for vain originality;
You should have regard only for inward nobility.

Reden

Wie kommt es, dass der Roten Wolke Wort
Über ein Erdending uns tief bewegt,
Während gestelzte Schulphilosophie
Wie Herbstlaub ist, vom Winde weggefegt?

Ein Schriftgelehrter sprach vor müdem Volk
Von Schriftendeutung und Theologie;
Nach ihm sprach Rūmī über seine Katz;
Ergriffen war die Menge wie noch nie.

Der Mensch, der zu euch dies und jenes sagt,
Ist manchmal wirklicher, als was er sagte;
Denn seine Größe gibt unendlich mehr
Als was er äußerlich zu reden wagte.

Wörter

Zwangsläufig nützt der Weise nur die Wörter
Die ihm die Sprache bietet. Und der Tor
Benützt die gleichen Wörter, nützt sie ab –
Hör nicht die Rede, schließe ihr dein Ohr.

Denn es kommt nicht auf Wörter an. So höre
Auf das, was sie bedeuten; wenn du sprichst,
Du schaust der Dinge Wesen. Das Gerede
Der Unbefugten – es bedeutet nichts.

Speaking

Why is it that a speech by Chief Red Cloud
About an earthly thing moves us deeply,
Whereas stilted school-philosophy
Is like dead leaves scattered by the wind?

A scholar spoke to a weary assembly
On scriptural exegesis and theology;
After him came Rūmī who spoke about his cat:
The crowd was moved as never before.

The person who says this or that to you
Is sometimes more real than what he said;
For his own greatness bestows infinitely more
Than what outwardly he dared to say.

Words

Of necessity, the wise man uses only the words
That language offers him. The fool
Uses the same words, but uses them up –
Do not listen to his speech, stop your ears.

For what counts are not the words. Listen
To what they mean; when you speak,
You look at the essence of things.
The chatter of the incompetent – it means nothing.

Was Gott liebt

Im Shintō ist die Reinlichkeit Gebot;
So auch für Hindus und Moslemen, und
Manch andre. Nicht für alle: manche denken
Unreinheit tue Gottesliebe kund –
Pflege des Leibes, Schönheit, seien Sünde,
Weil beides Lust und Weltlichkeit verkünde.
Der Buße und der Sitte Wüterich
Hat keinen Sinn für Gottes Werk an sich.

Es ist nicht sauber, stets Verdacht zu hegen;
Was Gott liebt, sollst du achten, folglich pflegen.

Schönheitssinn

Schön ist, was uns gefällt – so denken manche
Ganz fälschlich; denn man liebt das wirklich Schöne –
So man's versteht – weil schön es ist an sich,
Im Reich der Formen und im Reich der Töne.

Ganz anders ist die Frage der Verwandtschaft
Mit einer Art des Schönen: was du bist,
Das liebst du; und mit Recht, wenn du verstehst
Was jede, und was alle Schönheit ist.

What God Loves

In Shintō cleanliness is law;
It is the same for Hindus and Muslims
And many others. But not for all: some think
That uncleanliness shows love of God –
That care of the body and beauty are a sin,
Because they proclaim pleasure and worldliness.
The person obsessed with penance and morals
Has no sense of God's work in itself.

It is not clean always to harbor distrust;
What God loves, thou shouldst honor, and so cultivate.

Sense of Beauty

Beautiful is what pleases us – so some think,
Quite falsely; for one loves what is truly beautiful –
If one understands it – because it is beautiful in itself,
In the realm of forms and in the realm of sounds.

Quite another matter is the question of affinity
With a particular kind of beauty: you love
What you are; and rightly so, if you understand
What each and what all beauty is.

Stil

Die Griechenkunst zur Zeit des Perikles
Konnte die Form, doch kaum den Geist uns zeigen.
Bei andern Völkern zeigte sich der Sinn
Mehr als die Form; sie musst dem Geist sich beugen –
Daher der Stil, der stets die Form entstellt,
Doch Schönes gibt, weil er im Geist sich hält.

Schön ist der Venus Leib – nicht die Gebärde,
Die bürgerliche Scham verrät; indessen:
Schön sind der Lakschmī Bilder – mehr als Erde –
Da sie des Geistes goldne Trauben pressen.

Kunst ist nicht bloße Form, nicht Geist allein;
Weise Verbindung gibt den wahren Wein.

Klang und Stille

Musik ist Seele, Rhythmus, Melodie,
Inneres Spiel, das uns der Himmel lieh –

Und das sich wandelt, wie im Traum erneut:
In Schwermut, Leidenschaft und Seligkeit.

Der Saiten Zauber und des Menschen Sang –
Irdische Sehnsucht, himmlischer Empfang.

Dann wieder Stille – denn auch heilges Schweigen
Kann uns der Weisheit Wein und Schöne zeigen.

Style

Greek art at the time of Pericles
Could show us form, but scarcely Spirit.
With other peoples, meaning showed
More than form; form had to bow before the Spirit –
Whence a style that always distorts form,
Yet gives beauty, because it adheres to the Spirit.

The body of Venus is beautiful – not its gesture,
Which reveals conventional shame; whereas
Sculptures of Lakshmī are beautiful – more than earthly –
Because they press the Spirit's golden grapes.

Art is not mere form, nor is it Spirit alone;
A wise combination yields the true wine.

Sound and Stillness

Music is soul, rhythm and melody,
An inward play which Heaven lent to us –

And which transforms itself, as if renewed in dream,
Into melancholy, passion and bliss.

The magic sound of strings and human song –
Earthly longing, heavenly welcome.

Then stillness once again – for holy silence too
Can show us Wisdom's wine and beauty.

Entfaltung

Im Tanz entfaltet Schönheit Möglichkeiten,
So wie die Schöpfung Gottes Namen zeigt.
Musik ist Sprache des Ansich, des Seins,
Jenseits des Worts, das Innerstes verschweigt.

In Dichtung wird die Rede zur Musik,
Sie bietet beides, erst Begriff, dann Sein.
Tanz, Dichtung und Musik – sie stehn sich nah:
Das Wasser, wie in Kana, wird zu Wein.

Guter Rat

Tierbändiger – die sollte es nicht geben;
Denn auch die Tiere haben ihre Würde.
Wenn ihr die Leute unterhalten wollt,
Tut was ihr könnt und traget selbst die Bürde.

Das Tier fühlt wohl im Menschen Gottes Grund,
Kann eures Blicks Magie nicht widerstehen;
Doch macht kein gottvergessnes Spiel daraus –
Ihr sollt im Tier die Spur der Gottheit sehen.

Überlieferung

Nicht nur die Religion hat Gott gebracht –
Er hat auch deren Formentum gemacht.

Nicht können Denker Glaubenswelten gründen.
Auch eine Kunstwelt kann man nicht erfinden.

Dem Überlieferten bleibt zeitlos treu,
Auf dass die Umwelt nicht ein Blendwerk sei.

Denn wenn ihr nicht in wahren Formen lebt,
Ist außen nichts, was euch nach Oben hebt.

Unfolding

In dance, beauty unfolds its possibilities,
Just as creation manifests the Names of God.
Music is the language of the "As-Such," of Being,
Beyond words, which are silent about the most inward things.

In poetry, speech becomes music;
It offers both things: firstly concept, then being.
Dance, poetry and music — they are akin:
Water, as at Cana, is changed to wine.

Good Advice

Animal tamers — they should not exist;
For animals too have their dignity.
If you wish to entertain the crowd,
Do what you can and bear the burden yourselves.

Animals may well feel the divine kernel in man,
They cannot resist the magic of your gaze;
But do not make of this a God-forgetting play —
You should see in animals the trace of Divinity.

Tradition

God brought us not only religion —
He also ordained its particular form.

Thinkers cannot found religious worlds.
Nor can one invent a world of art.

Always stay faithful to what is traditional,
So that the ambience does not mislead you.

For if you do not live among true forms,
Nothing in the outward will lift you upwards.

Vom Islam

Jnāna und Bhakti – Weisheitsweg und Liebe –
Seltsam, dass Islams Dogma Jnāna ist,
Und dass im Islam die Philosophie
Neben der Mystik sich wie Jnāna liest.

Im Sufitum ist Bhakti wohl vorhanden –
Doch wirst du stets am Strand des Jnāna landen.
So der Prophet: er ist nicht von der Zunft
Der Bhaktas – er ist Urbild der Vernunft.

Wohl bergen Weisheit alle Religionen –
Die Frage ist, was sie im Wort betonen.

Vom Westen

Im Morgenland fällt die Idee ins Herz;
Im Abendlande bleibt sie im Gehirn;
So ist sie kaum ein Weg zum Seelenheil –
Sie kann Europas Knoten nicht entwirrn.

Das Schicksal wollt den Westen nicht berauben;
Es schenkte ihm des Ostens Schatz: den Glauben.
Jedoch die Weisheit hat nicht ganz zu schweigen;
Des sind Pythagoras und Plato Zeugen –

Ihr Geistesgut konnt blühn und sich verzweigen.

About Islam

Jnāna and *Bhakti* – the paths of wisdom and love –
Curious, that Islam's dogma is *jnāna*,
And that in Islam philosophy,
As well as mysticism, appear as *jnāna*.

In Sufism, *bhakti* is indeed present –
But you will always end up on *jnāna*'s shore.
So too the Prophet: he does not belong to the guild
Of *bhaktas* – he is the archetype of intelligence.

Certainly all religions contain wisdom –
The question is, what their language accentuates.

About the West

With Easterners, the idea falls into the heart;
With Westerners, it remains in the brain,
So it is hardly a way to salvation –
It cannot disentangle Europe's knots.

Destiny did not wish to deprive the West;
It gave it the Orient's treasure: faith.
But wisdom did not have to keep wholly silent;
Pythagoras and Plato are witness to this –

Their treasury of wisdom could bloom and spread.

Ikonostase

Die Glaubensheiligen in Religionen:
Ein jeder ist ein Sinnbild, ein Phänomen –
So wie ein Wunder, das Natur durchbricht;
Sie stehn im Glaubensraum mit goldnen Kronen.

Die „Narren Gottes" – nicht, dass man es übe;
Doch trinkt von ihrem Wein der Gottesliebe.

Eröffnung

Islam und Judentum verbieten Bilder –
Welche Verarmung, sagen die Pedanten.
Die Einschränkung – sie sehn es nicht – eröffnet
Uns manchen Weg, den wir zuvor nicht kannten.

Trinkest du Wasser, trinkst du keinen Wein;
Ein Ding kann nicht es selbst und andres sein.

Gerecht sein

Ihr wundert euch, dass Christen man verfolgte;
Man tat's nicht, weil sie an die Hostie glaubten.
Man tat es, weil ihr Glaube zwingen wollte –
Weil sie die Römer ihrer Welt beraubten.

Kaum war der Kaiser selber Christ geworden,
Konnt man die weise Frau Hypatia morden,
Auf dass von Plato nichts mehr übrig bliebe –
Was man vergaß, war Christi Nächstenliebe.
„Wer ohne Sünde, werf den ersten Stein" –
Sie glaubten sich von allen Sünden rein.

Iconostasis

The saints of faith in all religions:
Each one is a symbol, a phenomenon –
Like a miracle that breaks through Nature;
In the universe of faith they stand with golden crowns.

The "fools of God" – one should not imitate them;
But drink from the wine of their love of God.

Opening

Islam and Judaism prohibit images –
What an impoverishment, the pedants say.
The restriction – they do not see this – opens for us
Many a path we did not know before.

When thou drinkest water, thou drinkest not wine;
A thing cannot be itself and something else at the same time.

Being Just

You are surprised that the Christians were persecuted?
It was not because they believed in the sacred host.
It was because they sought to impose their belief –
Because they robbed the Romans of their world.

Barely had the emperor himself become a Christian
Than one could murder the wise Hypatia,
So that nothing more of Plato would remain –
What they forgot was Christ's love of the neighbor.
"He who is without sin, let him cast the first stone" –
They believed themselves to be free from all sin.

Heiliger Krieg

Die Glaubenseiferer, die sich bekämpfen,
Sie wissen nicht: es ist der gleiche Krieg
Auf Gottes Seite und für Gottes Reich.
Keiner verliert; es gibt nur Einen Sieg –

Den Sieg in uns, für Gott, – das äußre Schwert
Ist Sinnbild nur, das sich nach innen kehrt.

Audiat

Schiffbruch gemacht hab jede Religion –
So heißt es. Schiffbruch machte nur der Mensch;
Dass Religion verschwand, ist nur sein Lohn.

Die Religion, sagt man, sei unverständlich;
Taub ist man, wenn man nicht verstehen will;
Der Religionen Kern ist selbstverständlich.

Audiat – das Rad des Geistes steht nicht still.

Schlüsselbund

Das Allerheiligste hat viele Türen;
Der Hohepriester trägt den Schlüsselbund.
Der Meister kann des Schülers suchend Herz
Durch manche Tür zu Gottes Wohnsitz führen.

Der Schlüssel ist die Weisung, die den Geist
Erleuchtet und zum Wahren führt. Bedenke:
Vielseitig ist der Weg zum Heil. Es gibt
Gar manche Weine in der Wahrheit Schenke.

Holy War

The religious zealots who fight each other
Do not know: it is the same war
On God's side, and for God's Kingdom.
No one loses, there is only one victory –

The victory in us, for God – the outward sword
Is but a symbol that turns inward.

Audiat

All religions have shipwrecked – it is said.
But it is man alone that is shipwrecked;
The disappearance of religion is but his own reward.

Religion, they say, is incomprehensible.
Deaf is he who does not wish to understand;
The kernel of religion is self-evident.

Audiat – the Spirit's wheel does not stand still.

Ring of Keys

The Holy of Holies has many doors;
The high-priest carries the ring of keys.
The Master leads the disciple's questing heart
Through many a door to God's Mansion.

The key is the guidance that enlightens the mind
And brings it to the True. So reflect:
Manifold is the path to salvation. There are
Many wines in the tavern of Truth.

Hesychia

Die Hesychasten reden vom Zerschmelzen
Des Herzens: trink den Namen, sagen sie –
Der Name wird dich trinken. Ihre Mystik
Ist Stille in des Betens Melodie –
Im Taborlicht, das ihnen Gott verlieh.

Scheingeist

Jemand behauptete, Ātmā zu sein –
Der Guru hab gesagt: du musst es wissen,
Und das genügt. – So sprach zu mir ein Mann
In vollem Ernst. Die Stimmung war zerrissen –
Wie fortgeweht von einem Wirbelwind.
Mit Leuten red ich nicht, die Ātmā sind.

Doch: „Ich bin Ātmā, andres war ich nie" –
Gewiss. Die Frage stellt sich aber: Wie.

Philosophaster

Ein Vorurteil – so meinte jemand – sei
Zu glauben, nach dem Eins komme das Zwei;
Es sei ein Vorurteil, dass, was geschieht,
Aus einer Ursach sein Geschehen zieht.
Voraussetzungslos sei das rechte Denken –
Dann kann der Reiter seinen Gaul verschenken!

Es liegt im tiefsten Wesen aller Dinge,
Dass jedes seines Urbilds Loblied singe.

Hesychia

The Hesychasts speak of the melting of the heart:
Drink the Name, they say –
And the Name will drink thee. Their mysticism
Is silence within the melody of prayer –
In the light of Tabor, which God bestowed on them.

Hypocrisy

Someone thought that he was *Ātmā* –
His guru had supposedly told him: this thou must know,
And this suffices. – So said a man to me,
Completely in earnest. The atmosphere was ruptured –
As if swept away by a whirlwind.
I do not speak with people who are *Ātmā*.

Yet: "I am *Ātmā*, never was I other" –
Certainly. But the question is: How.

Philosophists

It is a prejudice – someone said – to believe
That after one comes two;
It is a prejudice to believe that what occurs
Draws its occurrence from a cause.
The right way to think is without presuppositions, they believe –
In that case, the rider can give away his horse!

It lies in the deep substance of all things
That each one sings the praise of its archetype.

Die Messung

Der Elefant ist groß, die Mücke klein –
Gelehrte sagen, dies sei bloßer Schein;
Kein Ding sei groß, kein Ding sei klein an sich;
Der Mensch nur sehe dies, gar wunderlich.

Sie irren sich; Gott wollte Klein und Groß;
Es sind ganz sinngemäße Wirklichkeiten.
Der Mensch ist Maßstab, deshalb ist er da;
Und es ist zwecklos, über dies zu streiten.

Zusatz

Ganz anders ist die Frage, wie wir messen
Was uns geschieht: ob Selbstsucht, Leidenschaft
Das Maß verfälscht. Wenn man Erlebtes misst,
Soll man den Wunsch des Messenden vergessen.

Die Welt ist klein – sie ist dem Schöpfer fern;
Es gibt nur Eine Größe – die des Herrn.

Populus

Ist es nicht reichlich sinnlos, einer Sache
Nützen zu wollen, wenn sie nutzlos ist?
Ist nicht das Volk ein hundertköpfger Drache,
Wenn es den Sinn des Menschentums vergisst?

Kenntnis des Wesentlichen ist vonnöten –
Vox Dei ist das Volk in seinem Beten.

Measure

The elephant is big, the fly is small –
Scientists say that this is mere appearance;
That in itself no thing is big or small;
Man merely sees it so, most strangely.

They are wrong; God wanted small and big;
They correspond entirely to realties.
Man is the measure – that is why he exists,
And it is useless to quarrel over this.

Addendum

Quite other is the question how we measure
What befalls us: whether self-seeking or passion
Falsifies our measure. When one measures an experience,
One should forget the wishes of the measurer.

The world is small – far from the Creator;
There is but one greatness – that of the Lord.

Populus

Is it not wholly meaningless to wish
To be of use to a cause that is itself useless?
Is not the people a many-headed dragon,
When it forgets the meaning of the human condition?

Knowledge of the essential is indispensable –
The people is *Vox Dei* when it prays.

Ich möchte

Ich möcht mich nur mit Heiligem befassen –
Muss manchmal niedersteigen in die Gassen
Menschlicher Kleinheit, die nicht nichtsein kann;
Selig, der Siege über sich gewann!

Du hättest gern, dass man dir Beifall zollte –
Groß bist du nur in dem, was Gott dir wollte.

Vom Menschen

Der Mensch ist Erde, steht dem Tiere nah,
Und ist doch Geist; er muss die Tierheit tragen,
Will sie vergessen, sie unkenntlich machen,
Und muss sich doch mit ihr durchs Leben plagen.

Vergeistigt ist die Tierform; unser Leib
Und unser Antlitz sind von Gott die Zeugen
Und fordern Seelenadel – Geisteskräfte
Die, ihrem Wesen treu, zum Urbild steigen.

Der Mensch kann irren, fallen von der Höhe –
Das edle Tier ist besser als der Böse.
Gott der Erbarmer strahlet in die Welt,
Auf dass sein Wort sein Ebenbild erlöse.

I Would Like

I would like to deal only with sacred things –
But I must sometimes descend into the byways
Of human pettiness, which cannot not be;
Blessèd is he who has won victories over himself!

Thou wouldst like that someone give thee praise –
Thou art great only in that which God willed for thee.

About Man

Man is earth, close to the animal,
And yet he is spirit; he must bear the burden of animality,
He wishes to forget it, to make it unrecognizable,
And yet he must suffer with it throughout his life.

The animal form is spiritualized;
Our body and our face bear witness to God
And demand nobility of soul – spiritual forces
Which, true to their nature, ascend to the archetype.

Man can err and fall from his height –
The noble animal is better than the wicked man.
God the Merciful shines into the world,
So that His Word may liberate His likeness.

A perpetuo succursu

So wie die Engel, haben hohe Menschen
Im Paradies die Fähigkeit, zu hören
Was tausend Erdenmenschen ihnen sagen
Zu gleicher Zeit, und lassen sich nicht stören
Durch diesen Andrang.
So Maria, die
Zu jeder Stund man anruft auf der Erde;
Gott will, dass unsres Erdendaseins Not
Durch einen Himmelsstrahl gelindert werde.

A perpetuo succursu

Like the angels, high souls in Paradise
Have the capacity to hear
What thousands of men on earth say to them
At the same time, without being disturbed
By this throng.
                    Such is Mary,
Who is invoked on earth at every hour;
God wishes that the plight of our earthly existence
Be soothed by a ray from Heaven.

IV

Seele

~

The Soul

Der Pneumatiker

Der Alltagsmensch, der auf das Äußre schaut,
Kann den Verinnerlichten kaum verstehen;
Des Adel ist, der Dinge Kern zu schauen –
Im Menschen stets das Gottesbild zu sehen.

Denn auf die tiefe Absicht kommt es an –
Manches mag seltsam, oberflächlich scheinen
Weil man nicht weiß, dass in des Weisen Geist
Die Formen sich mit ihrem Grund vereinen.

Dem Toren ist die Welt des Lebens Ziel;
Dem Weisen ist sie wie ein Maskenspiel.

Vollmond

So wie der Vollmond in der Sterne Meer –
So Krishna, wenn die Gopis ihn umringen;
Was ist wohl seliger: die Mitte sein
Oder, im Kreise, Krishnas Lob zu singen?

Der Vollmond leuchtet nicht von eignem Licht –
Sein Leuchten ist geschenkt, es kommt von oben.
So ist auch Krishnas goldner Strahlenkranz
Aus Mahadevas Gotteslicht gewoben.

Pneumatikos

The ordinary man, who looks at the outward,
Can hardly understand one who is interiorized;
Whose nobility is to gaze upon the kernel of things –
To see in man the image of God.

For what counts is the profound intention –
Much may seem strange or superficial
Because one does not know that in the wise man's mind
Forms are united with their essence.

For the fool, the world is the goal of life;
For the wise, it is like a play of masks.

Full Moon

Like the full moon in the sea of stars –
Such is Krishna, when the *gopīs* surround him.
Which is more blissful: to be the center,
Or, in the circle, to sing Krishna's praise?

The full moon does not shine with its own light –
Its shining is a gift, it comes from Above.
So too is Krishna's golden crown of rays
Woven of Mahādeva's divine Light.

Probleme

Gott will das Übel, denn sonst wär es nicht;
Er will es irgendwie, doch wünscht es nicht.
Er lässt geschehn, doch straft den Bösewicht;
Er will, was sein muss, dennoch hält Gericht.

Unendlichkeit: was möglich, muss geschehen,
Und niemand kann das Weltrad rückwärts drehen.
Böses ist nur ein Funke in dem All
Das sein will; denn das Gut ist überall.

Böses muss sein, weil manches große Gut
Auf einem Sieg der guten Macht beruht:
So die Befreiung aus des Leidens Banden,
Die es nicht gäb, wär Böses nicht vorhanden.

Du sollst es wissen, und nicht bloß vermuten:
Das Böse ist der Sauerteig des Guten;
Beziehungsweise. Dies ist wesentlich:
Das Gute ist Vollkommenheit in sich.

Das Gute webt die Welt, mit allem Schein;
Was schlecht man nennt, ist nicht der Dinge Sein.

Problems

God wills evil, otherwise it would not exist;
He wills it in some way; yet does not wish it.
He allows it to happen, but punishes the evil-doer;
He wills what has to be, yet sits in judgment.

Infinity: what is possible must occur,
And no one can reverse the world-wheel's spinning.
Evil is merely a spark in the All
That wills to be; for the good is everywhere.

Evil must exist, for often a great good
Comes from a victory of the good's power:
Thus, deliverance from the bonds of suffering
Would not be possible if evil did not exist.

This thou must know and not merely suppose:
Evil is the leaven of the good,
In a relative way. This is essential:
The Good is perfection in itself.

The Good weaves the world with all its appearances;
What one calls bad is not the true being of things.

Sehweise

Das Übel, das wir als Konkretes sehen,
Kann unser Alltagsdenken nicht verstehen.
Das Böse können wir abstrakt erfassen –
Dann können wir's dem Weltrad überlassen.

Und ähnlich: dass wir das sind, was wir sind,
Scheint selbstverständlich – nicht nur für das Kind.
Doch logisch können wir es kaum begreifen,
Dass wir uns in ein eignes Ich versteifen.

Auch dieses: eines schönen Liedes wegen
Lässt sich die Seel aufs Innigste bewegen.
Der reine Geist in unsrer tiefen Brust
Ist sich, im Lied, stets seiner selbst bewusst.

Einheitlich ist das Weltbild, das wir bauen –
Verschieden unser Blick, mit dem wir schauen.
Wir sehen, dass die Dinge sind, und fließen –
Doch andrerseits: warum sie da sein müssen.

Der Blick, um den die Rätselwelt sich schart,
Ist mit der Weisheit Einheitsblick gepaart.

Der Kaufpreis

Daran, dass man das große Glück nicht findet,
Will man sich rächen; und der Geist erblindet
Aus eitler Rachsucht. Sucht die Seligkeit
Dort, wo sie ist – jenseits von Raum und Zeit:

Im reinen Sein – vom Seinsquell kommt ihr her;
Im reinen Geist – Befreiung ist das Meer.
Hoch ist das Ziel; niedrig – ein zeitlich Ding –
Ist unsre Not. Der Kaufpreis ist gering.

Viewpoints

The evil that we see as something concrete,
Our everyday thinking cannot understand.
We can comprehend evil abstractly –
Then we can leave it to the world-wheel.

Likewise: that we are what we are
Seems self-evident – and not only to a child.
But logically we can hardly comprehend
That we are frozen into one particular ego.

This too: for the sake of a beautiful song,
The soul lets itself be moved to the very core.
The pure Spirit in our deepest breast is,
In the song, always conscious of itself.

Coherent is the world-image that we build –
Diverse is the gaze with which we see.
We see that things are, and that they flow –
Yet on the other hand, why they must exist.

The gaze that is surrounded by the world of riddles
Is paired with the unifying gaze of Wisdom.

The Price to Pay

One wishes to avenge oneself because one has not found
The great happiness; and the mind is blinded
By a vain desire for vengeance. Seek beatitude
Where it is to be found – beyond space and time:

In pure Being – you come from Being's source;
In the pure Spirit – deliverance is the sea.
High is the goal; low – a temporal thing –
Is our misery. The price to pay is insignificant.

Erlösung

Was uns erlöst? Für manche ein Messias –
Der feste Glaube an das Wunderbare.
Für andre Das, was ist – Bewusstsein dessen,
Des Wesen uns befreit: das Eine, Wahre.

Gewiss: die Wege sind nicht nur getrennt;
In jedem findet ihr, was ihr schon kennt.

Gegenüber

Weisheit und Liebestiefe: Er und Sie.
Musik und Metaphysik sind die Pole
Die, meint man, restlos auseinanderstreben;
Mitnichten. Beider Sein und Harmonie
Sind, was sie sind, dem Menschenherz zum Wohle –
Sind vorgezeichnet in der Gottheit Leben.
Beider Synthese ist der Wahrheit Liebe –
Und jeder Pol ist Außen und ist Innen
Und will sein eigen tiefstes Sein gewinnen.

Im Weisen

Der Adler und die Eule – Archetypen
Die sich im Geist des Weisen gern verbrüdern:
Die Eule will des Adlers Geistesblitz
Mit sinnender Beschaulichkeit erwidern;
Sie beide liebte man als Himmelssöhne –
Geweiht dem Vishnu, der Pallas Athene.

Des Geistes Schwert durchschneidet alle Zeit –
Das Ruhn im Sein schaut in die Ewigkeit.

Deliverance

What delivers us? For many, a Messiah –
The firm belief in the miraculous.
For others, That which is – consciousness of That,
Whose essence makes us free: the One, the True.

Certainly: the paths are not only distinct;
In each of them you find what you already know.

Face to Face

Wisdom and depth of Love: He and She.
Music and metaphysics are two poles
Which, according to some, entirely diverge;
Not at all. The existence and harmony of both
Are what they are for the good of man's heart –
They are prefigured in the Life of the Divinity.
The synthesis of both is love of Truth –
And each pole is the outward and the inward,
And seeks to reach its own inmost being.

In the Wise Man

The eagle and the owl – archetypes
That in the wise man's spirit gladly become brothers:
The owl responds to the eagle's flash of spirit
With meditative contemplativity;
Both were beloved as Heaven's sons –
Consecrated to Vishnu and to Pallas Athena.

The Spirit's sword cuts through all time –
Repose in Being looks into Eternity.

Pax Domini

Der Mensch: nach rechts und links und auf und ab –
So ist sein Wünschen und so ist sein Leben
Von seiner Kindheit bis zu seinem Grab.

Nach außenhin, ins Andre, ist sein Streben –
Sei du zufrieden in des Herzens Mitte,
Die alles in sich fasst. Der Herr ist nah –
Wo das Gebet, ist Gottes Gegenwart;

Gibt es ein Glück auf Erden, ist es da.

Intra vos

Innerlichkeit. Leben nach Innen, denn:
Gottesgewissheit, Heilsgewissheit wohnen
Im tiefsten Herzen. Glaube und Gebet –
Sie wird der Herr mit Seligkeit belohnen;
Regnum caelorum autem intra vos.

Nicht Zweifel – Glaube macht die Seele groß.
Vermutung ist Gedankenwerk; allein
Des Geistes Urgewissheit ist ein Sein.

Bleiben, Werden

Bleib, was du bist, und dennoch werde mehr;
Gewiss, du wirst kein König und kein Kaiser.
Du warst ein Kind, und es war Gutes dran;
Behalte es getrost, doch werde weiser.

Sein, was man war; die Kindheit tut uns wohl.
Mehr noch: sei auch der edle Gegenpol.

Pax Domini

Man: to the right and left, and up and down –
Thus is his wishing and thus is his life,
From childhood unto the grave.

Towards the outward, into the other, is his striving –
Be content in thy heart's center
Which contains everything. The Lord is near –
Where there is prayer, there is God's Presence;

If there is a Happiness on earth, it is here!

Intra vos

Inwardness. To live towards the inward, because:
Certitude of God and certitude of salvation
Dwell within the deepest heart. Faith and prayer –
The Lord will reward them with bliss;
Regnum caelorum autem intra vos.

Not doubt, but faith makes the soul great.
Speculation is the activity of thought;
Only the pure certitude of the Spirit is being.

Remaining, Becoming

Remain what thou art, and yet become more;
Of course, thou wilt not become king or emperor.
Thou wast a child, and there was good in this;
Preserve this with trust, but become wiser.

To be what one was; childhood does us good.
Yet there is more: be also the noble counterpart.

El-Allaui

So sprach der Scheich: Was not tut auf dem Pfad,
Das ist der Wunsch, sich selbst zu übersteigen.
Unheilbar ist, wer diesen Wunsch nicht hat;
Wer Allāh hören will, des Herz muss schweigen.

Höhenflug

Du möchtest wie ein Adler aufwärts fliegen
Zum Licht der Wahrheit, das die Seel befreit;
Wundre dich nicht: da ist die Erdenmacht
Die dir dein Aufwärtssteigen nicht verzeiht.

Sie sucht dir die Befreiung zu behindern
Mit allen Mitteln, großen und auch kleinen;
Kümmre dich nicht! Tu immer, was du kannst –
Gott wird die Seele mit dem Licht vereinen.

Der Inhalt

Er wolle dieses Leben voll genießen,
Sagte mir jemand. Stellt sich nur die Frage:
Ist dieses Lebens Inhalt der Genuss,
Oder ist rechtes Leben fromme Plage.

Nein, rechtes Leben ist das Glück der Pflicht:
Denn jeder Mensch hat einen Wert zu geben –
Dann hat er Recht auf manche edle Freud;
Jedoch das Wesentliche ist das Streben –

Mit ihm die Hoffnung, dass sich das erfülle,
Was in der Ewigkeit des Schöpfers Wille.

Al-'Alawī

Thus spoke the Shaykh: what is necessary on the Path
Is the desire to transcend oneself.
Incurable is he who does not have this desire;
Who wishes to hear Allāh, his heart must be silent.

Flying to the Heights

Thou wishest to soar upwards like an eagle
To the light of Truth that frees the soul;
Do not wonder that there is the earth's power,
That does not forgive thee thine ascent.

It tries to prevent thy deliverance
By any means, great or small;
Be not troubled! Do always what thou canst —
God will unite thy soul with His Light.

The Content

He wanted to enjoy this life to the full,
Someone told me. But the question arises:
Is the content of this life enjoyment,
Or is right living a pious ordeal?

Nay, right living is the happiness of duty:
For every man has something of value to give —
Then he has the right to many a noble pleasure;
But the essential is the striving —

And with it the hope that there be fulfilled
What in eternity is the Creator's Will.

Abwehr

Gewisse Wahnideen kannst du kennen
Erst wenn umständehalber sie sich nennen.
Deshalb ist wesentlich, dass jede Seite
Der Seele wahren Edelmut verbreite.

Der Böse niemals in die Seele dringt
In welcher Gottes Gegenwart erklingt.
Er mag auch Gottesfreunde etwas schinden –
Er kann in ihnen keine Wohnung finden.

Meisterschaft

Der Derwisch, welcher keinen Meister hat,
Des Meister ist der Teufel, sagt die Lehre.
Wes Schüler ist der Meister selber, der
Allein steht? Intellekt – er hat die Ehre.

Aliquid increatum – reiner Geist
Im tiefsten Herzen. Was beweist sein Licht?
Die Gotteswahrheit, die von Innen leuchtet –
Du kennst dich selber, oder kennst dich nicht.

Sich bescheiden

Man kann Gott immer um Erleuchtung bitten;
Man kann Ihn nicht zu einer Weisung zwingen.
Orakelkunst, Wahrsagerei, Erträumen –
All dies gehört wohl zu den schlimmsten Dingen.

Sei dir der Grenzen der Natur bewusst
Und überfrage nicht; tu was du musst.

Defense

Some delusive ideas you can recognize only when,
Because of circumstance, they show themselves.
Therefore it is essential that every aspect
Of the soul should radiate true nobility.

The evil one never penetrates the soul
In whom God's Presence resounds.
Even if he may somewhat ill-treat God's friends –
He can find no dwelling-place in them.

Mastership

The dervish who has no master
Has the devil for master, so it is taught.
Whose disciple is the Master himself,
Who stands alone? The Intellect – it has the honor.

Aliquid increatum – pure Spirit
In the deepest heart. What proves its light?
God's Truth, which shines from within –
Either thou knowest thyself, or thou knowest thyself not.

Being Contented

One can always ask God for enlightenment;
One cannot force Him to give an instruction.
Oracles, fortune-telling, dream-mongering –
All these belong to the very worst of things.

Be conscious of nature's limits,
And do not over-ask; do what thou must.

Lernen

Nicht dass man seinen Eltern böse wäre –
Doch manche ihrer Fehler wirkten weiter
Im Leben, und dies kann man nicht vergessen;
Doch Deo gratias wird das Herz gescheiter.
Verzeihen oder Zorn ist nicht die Frage;
Der Dinge Gründe sehn ist keine Klage.

Wir können kaum mit Gottes Maßen messen –
Doch Gottesliebe macht die Seele heiter.

Im Grund

Vergangenheit – wir könnten auch vergessen.
Der Mensch will sich erinnern; jedoch wessen?
Erinnerung – das, was wir in ihr lieben,
Steht irgendwie im Ewigen geschrieben.
Durch das Geliebte schau hindurch und höre –
Zur Erde dringt der Strahl der Engelschöre.
Wir sind geboren aus dem Geisteswind –
Wir lieben das, was wir im Grunde sind.

Justitia

Ein jeder Mensch muss in der Lage sein
Das, was sein Stand erfordert, zu erfüllen.
Dies ist Gerechtigkeit: mach es ihm leicht,
Wenn immer möglich; er soll seinen Willen –
In Gottes Namen – widmen seinen Pflichten.

Gerecht ist, dass wir unser Werk verrichten;
Gerecht ist nicht, dass ich der Andre sei;
Wir sind verschieden. Es ist einerlei
Ob schwer, ob leicht. Der Höchste wird uns richten.

Learning

Not that one wishes to blame one's parents –
But some of their errors continue to have effect
In life, and this one cannot forget;
Yet, *Deo gratias*, the heart becomes wiser.
Forgiveness or anger is not the question;
Seeing the cause of things is not to complain.

We can hardly measure with God's measures –
But love of God cheers the soul.

In our Depth

The past – we could also forget.
Man wishes to remember, but what?
Remembrance – what we love in it,
Is somehow written in eternity.
Look deeply through what thou lovest, and listen –
The ray of the angels' choir reaches the earth.
We are born from the wind of the Spirit –
We love what we are in our depth.

Justitia

Every man must be in a position
To accomplish what his station in life requires.
This is justice: make it easy for him
Whenever possible; he must – in the Name of God –
Dedicate his will to his duties.

It is just that we accomplish our work;
It is not just, that I be someone else;
We are different. It matters not
Whether it be difficult or easy. The Most High will judge us.

Zu unterscheiden

In jeder Menschenseele gibt es Pole,
Die sich ergänzen und in Eintracht leben.
Im bösen Wesen wirken Gegensätze,
Die, sich nicht kennend, auseinanderstreben.

Kindlich Gemüt gehört gar oft dem Weisen,
Und stark mag sein das scheinbar schwache Weib.
Doch mit zwei Seelen Leute zu betrügen,
Dies ist – umsonst – des Bösen Zeitvertreib.

Mag ein gespaltnes, schlechtes Ich uns kränken –
Die edle Seel wird doppelt uns beschenken.

Mögliches

Umgang mit Narren macht den Klugen wirr –
Wer mag es sein, der den Verstand verliert?
Jedoch: was möglich ist, kann nicht nichtsein;
Versteh, dass dein Verdruss zu nichts dich führt.

Allmöglichkeit: du kannst ihr Sein erfassen;
Ihr Einzelnes will sich nicht zählen lassen.

Sendung

Man muss so manches in der Menschheit rügen –
Man möchte lieber Gutes anerkennen.
Doch man hat keine Wahl: der Mensch ist Mensch;
Wer Wahrheit lehrt, muss mancherlei verbrennen –

Und manches loben. So trifft keinen Tadel
Den, dessen Sendung ist der Wahrheit Adel.

To Distinguish

In every human soul there are poles
Which complement each other and live in harmony.
In the wicked person oppositions are at work
Which, not knowing each other, draw apart.

A childlike nature often belongs to the wise man,
And strong may be the seemingly frail woman.
But with two souls to deceive other people,
This is — in vain — the pastime of the wicked.

A fissured and bad ego may injure us —
The noble soul will reward us doubly.

What is Possible

To associate with fools bewilders the intelligent —
Who might be the one to lose his mind?
However: what is possible cannot not be;
Understand that thy vexation leads thee nowhere.

All-Possibility: thou canst understand its being;
But its particulars cannot be numbered.

Mission

One has to criticize so much in humanity —
One would prefer to acknowledge the good.
But one has no choice, for man is man;
Who teaches the Truth, must burn many things —

And must praise many things. Thus no blame falls
On him whose mission is the nobility of Truth.

Hinzugefügt

An sich ist lobenswert, dass alle Menschen
In einem Seelenwinkel Gutes tragen;
Keiner ist bloß aus bösem Stoff gemacht –
Doch nützt es keinem Menschen, es zu sagen.

Der Knoten

Verzicht auf Rache ist gewiss nicht Schwäche;
Geheime Rachsucht ist gewiss nicht Stärke;
„Mein ist die Rache, spricht der Herr." Sieh zu:
Im Friedensgeist vollbringe deine Werke.

Das, was dir schädlich ist, kannst du nicht wollen;
Auch sollst du nicht für nichts dem Nächsten grollen.
Die Seel soll über Gordions Knoten schweben
In Dankbarkeit – dann wird ihr Gott vergeben.

Antworten

Sagt ja zum Leben – lasst das Denken fallen;
So sagt der Weltnarr in des Teufels Krallen.

So soll Verneinung unsre Haltung sein?
Durchaus nicht; sagt zum Leben: ja und nein.

Sagt ja, wenn ihr das Sein durchs Dasein seht;
Sagt nein, wenn euch zu lieb ist, was vergeht.

Added

It is in itself praiseworthy that every man,
In a corner of his soul, has some good;
No man is made solely of bad substance –
But it helps no one to say so.

The Knot

To renounce vengeance is certainly not weakness;
Secret vengefulness is certainly not strength;
"Vengeance is Mine, saith the Lord." Take heed:
Accomplish thy work in the spirit of peace.

Thou dost not desire what is harmful for thyself;
Nor shouldst thou harbor vain resentment for thy neighbor.
The soul should soar above the Gordian knot
In gratitude – then will the Lord forgive her.

Answers

Say yes to life – leave thinking by the wayside;
Thus speaks the worldly fool caught in the devil's claws.

So, should our attitude be negation?
By no means; say to life: yes and no.

Say yes, when, through existence, you see Being;
Say no, when you are too fond of things that fade.

Kleingröße

Der beste Weg, verfälscht und klein zu werden
Ist dieser Wunsch: der Größte sein auf Erden –
Und zu vergessen, dass die Größe nur
Ein Strahl sein kann von göttlicher Natur.

Oft muss man hören, Hochmut sei die Sünde
Des Weisen, der sein Wissen göttlich finde.
Eitel ist nur, wer sich ins Ich verrennt;
Nicht, dessen Geist der Ichheit Trug verbrennt.

Größe ist nicht, was bloßer Ehrgeiz machte –
Groß kann nur sein, was Gott vom Himmel brachte.

Frömmigkeit

Sinn für das Heilige, Andacht vor Gott;
Des Dieners Bangigkeit ist nicht das Gleiche.
Gott nimmt sie an von jenem, der sie übt –
Man nannte dies: Gehorsam einer Leiche.

So fragt nicht, wer Gott am meisten liebt –
Noch wen Er mehr als andre liebt; versteht:
Gar manche Wohnung ist in seinem Reiche –

Er weiß, wo jedes Herz geschrieben steht.

Leben

Sinneseindrücke will der Mensch genießen –
So geht das Leben spielend in der Runde
In einem nimmermüden Hin und Her –
Und dann auf einmal naht die letzte Stunde
Mit ihrer Nacht. Doch macht euch keine Sorgen –

Die Liebe Gottes bringt den goldnen Morgen.

Small-Greatness

The best way to become falsified and small
Is this desire: to be the greatest one on earth –
And to forget that greatness
Can only be a ray of the Divine Nature.

One is often obliged to hear that pride is the sin
Of the sage, who deems his wisdom divine.
Only he is vain who is caught in his own ego,
Not he whose spirit burns up the illusion of egoity.

Greatness is not what mere ambition makes –
Only what God brings from Heaven can be great.

Piety

Sense of the sacred and devotion before God;
The fear of the servant is not the same as this.
God accepts it from the one who practices it –
It has been called: the obedience of a corpse.

So ask not who loves God the most –
Nor whom God loves more than others; understand:
Many indeed are the mansions in His Kingdom –

God knows where each heart is inscribed.

Life

Man wishes to enjoy sense impressions –
So life goes playing round and round
In a tireless to-and-fro –
Then suddenly the last hour draws near
With its night. Yet be not troubled –

Love of God brings the golden dawn.

Müssen

Ihr fühlt wohl kaum die Kleinheit eures Müssens –
Ihr gleitet wie an einer Schnur gezogen
Durch Raum und Zeit, und anders könnt ihr nicht –
Die Größe habt ihr selbst hineingelogen.

Wahr ist es: ihr seid frei, tut was ihr wollt;
Doch kleines Müssen ist hineingewoben
In euer stolzes Tun. Man fühlt sich stark,
Bewundernswert. Man wird herumgeschoben.

Gewiss, es ist nicht schändlich, dass wir müssen;
Doch wir sind umso freier, wenn wir's wissen.
Wir können es in unsrem Geiste lesen:
Freiheit des Urseins – unser tiefstes Wesen.

Wie können wir?

Wie können wir dem Dämon Zeit entrinnen?
Lasst doch die Parzen ganz alleine spinnen
Und bleibt, wo euch der Höchste hingesetzt:
In Gottgedenkens goldnem Jetzt.

Ausgleich

Des Daseins Mechanismus zu zergliedern
Ohne den Ausgleich eines innern Ja,
Würde die Seel zermürben; lasst sie leben
Vom Lichte, das der Geist im Einen sah.

Ein jedes Ding ist vielfach aufgebaut;
Wohl dem, der auf den Einen Sinn vertraut.

Compulsion

You scarcely feel the pettiness of your compulsions –
You glide along as if drawn on a string
Through space and time, and cannot do otherwise –
You have yourselves falsified greatness.

It is true: you are free, you do what you will;
Yet petty compulsions are woven
Into your haughty conduct. One feels strong
And admirable. But one is pushed this way and that.

Certainly, it is not disgraceful to be compelled;
But we are all the freer if we are conscious of it.
We can read this in our spirit:
Freedom of primordial Being – our essence most profound.

How can we?

How can we escape the demon time?
Leave the Fates to their spinning,
And remain where the Most High has placed you:
In the golden Now of God-remembrance.

Compensation

To dissect the mechanism of existence
Without the compensation of an inner "yes,"
Crushes the soul; let her live
By the Light that the spirit sees in the One.

Each thing is multifariously constructed;
Blessèd is he who trusts in the One Meaning.

Beherrschung

Ohn Selbstbeherrschung ist kein Edelmut;
Der Edle muss die Selbstbeherrschung üben
Aus Liebe – nicht für andre, nicht als Zwang;
Sie ist in seinen Seelenstoff geschrieben.

Er liebt sie, weil sie schön und sinnvoll ist;
Weil er nicht Schwäche, noch den Sieg vergisst.

Vom Adel

Edles Gehabe, das nur außen ist,
Ist weit entfernt von wahrem Edelmut.
Gewiss, der Edle zeigt stets Vornehmheit;
Ohn Adel ist der Kerl, der nur so tut.

Edles Gemüt findest du überall:
Beim Herrn im Schloss, beim Knecht im Pferdestall.
Der Seelenadel ist ein tiefes Sein;
Verächtlich ist der aufgeblasne Schein.

Nicht weltlich ist des wahren Adels Kern;
Er ist im Geist – er ist ein Strahl vom Herrn.

Gleichgewicht

Erkenntnis, Liebe; Kälte, Wärme – beide
Verbinden sich zu einer weisen Seele.
Dann auch der Friede und mit ihm die Freude –
Ruhe, Bewegung, dass dem Herz nichts fehle.

In jedem dieser Pole wohnt das Licht,
Mit ihm die Seligkeit; und unser Leben
Aufwärts zu Gott, der unser Urgrund ist
Und dessen Strahlen unser Dasein weben.

Mastery

There is no nobility without self-mastery;
The noble man must dominate himself
Out of love — not for others, not as constraint;
It is inscribed in the substance of his soul.

He loves it for its beauty and its meaning;
Because he forgets neither weakness nor victory.

On Nobility

Noble airs that are merely outward
Are far removed from true nobility.
Certainly, the noble man always manifests refinement;
The churl who merely feigns it is without nobility.

A noble disposition you can find everywhere:
With the lord in the castle, with the servant in the stable.
Nobility of soul is a profound being;
Inflated pretense is despicable.

The core of true nobility is not worldly;
It is in the spirit — it is a ray from the Lord.

Equilibrium

Knowledge and love; coldness and warmth —
Both combine to shape a wise man's soul.
Then also peace and with it joy —
Stillness and motion, that the heart may lack nothing.

In each of these poles dwells light,
And with it bliss; and our life
Upwards to God, Who is our First Cause
And Whose rays weave our existence.

Synthesis

Synthese, Analyse: du wirst traurig
Wenn dein Verstand das Weltall hat zerpflückt;
Du brauchst Synthese, denn sie ist dein Geist,
Der deine Seel erleuchtet und beglückt.

Bewahr, dass aus dem Fisch ein Vogel werde;
Jeder für sich – doch beide sind aus Erde.
Die Analyse will, dass Vielheit scheine;
Synthese kommt zuerst.
Gott ist der Eine.

Sechs Gedanken

Sechs Leitgedanken hat der Geist gegeben:
Enthaltung, Tat, Zufriedenheit, Vertrauen,
Erkenntnis, Selbstheit; andres brauchst du nicht.
Auf jeden Punktes Weisheit kannst du bauen.

Schwermut, Bitterkeit und Verzweiflung sind
Des Teufels Gifte, die den Mensch zerstören.
Des Geistes Freude, Milde, Sicherheit
Sind Himmelsboten, und du sollst sie hören.

Such nicht die Ruh in Dingen, welche schwanken;
Des Lebens Glück – es liegt in sechs Gedanken.

Synthesis

Synthesis, analysis: you grow sad
When your mind has picked apart the universe;
You need synthesis, for it is your spirit,
Which enlightens and gladdens your soul.

Take care that a fish not become a bird;
Each is distinct – though both are of the earth.
Analysis wishes the multiple to shine;
Synthesis comes first.
For God is the One.

Six Thoughts

The Spirit has given six guiding thoughts:
Renunciation, Act, Contentment, Trust,
Knowledge, Selfhood; thou needest nothing more.
On the wisdom of each point thou canst rely.

Melancholy, bitterness and despair
Are the devil's poisons, which destroy man.
The Spirit's joy, gentleness and security
Are messengers from Heaven, and thou shouldst heed them.

Do not seek rest in things that change;
Life's happiness – it lies in these six thoughts.

Gebe Gott

In unsrer Kindheit wähnen wir, die Welt
Sei ganz in Ordnung, lustig sei das Leben;
Im Alter sehen wir: die Welt ist krank;
Und was sie bieten kann, sind saure Reben.

Die Schrift hat uns belehrt vom Sündenfall:
Ein Fluch beschattet alle Erdendinge
Und unsre Seelen. Rette sich, wer kann –
Und gebe Gott, dass uns das Werk gelinge.

Kannst du im Geist verwandeln Blei zu Gold,
Dann ist dir auch der Schicksalsengel hold.

Man frägt

Man frägt, wie es im Himmel sei –
Das kann kein Erdenwesen wissen.
Und überdies – die Sach ist einerlei;
Im Himmel kann man nichts vermissen.

Sagt nicht, der Weise widerspreche sich
Weil er nicht immer sagt, was ihr erwartet.
Denn alles kommt auf die Beziehung an
In welcher er ein gleiches Ding betrachtet.

God Grant

In our childhood we fancy the world
Is all in order and life is merry;
But in old age we see: the world is ill,
And what it can offer are sour grapes.

Scripture has taught us about the Fall:
A curse hangs like a shadow over all earthly things
And our souls. Let him save himself who can –
And God grant that our work may succeed.

If in the spirit thou canst change lead to gold,
Then destiny's angel will also favor thee.

One Wonders

One wonders how it is in Heaven –
This no earthly creature can know.
And besides – the question is pointless;
In Heaven one will want for nothing.

Say not that the wise man contradicts himself
Because he does not always say what you expect.
For everything depends on the viewpoint
From which he considers the selfsame thing.

Stolz

Ein Grande Spaniens, sagt man, bückt sich nicht
Wenn ihm ein Goldstück auf den Boden fällt.
Denn ein Marquese bückt sich nicht für Geld;
Er bückt sich nur vor Gottes Angesicht;

Vor der Madonna – dann vor edlen Frauen,
Und vor des Königs zornbereiten Brauen.
Für Gold könnt er sich bücken, wenn er dächte:
Gott sieht dich – du bist einer seiner Knechte.

Denkt nicht, ihr seid zu gut für kleine Werte
Die euch der Herr für euer Wohl bescherte.
Wenn Goldauflesen unter eurem Stande,
Was suchtet ihr in Eldorados Lande?

Hochmut

Es gibt gerechten Stolz, sogar beim Weisen;
Der Stolze kann vor Gott in Demut leben.
Gerechten Hochmut hat es nie gegeben;
Denn Hochmut heißt zur Bitterkeit entgleisen.

Stolz ist oft edel – manchmal lächerlich;
Hochmut ist eine Teufelei an sich.

Demut

Schrieb Ibn Arabī: Die Demut ist
Zu kostbar, als dass sie zur Schau getragen;
Der Sufi übt sie innerlich für Gott –
Gleichviel, was Leute auf dem Markte sagen.

Pride

A Spanish grandee, it is said, would never stoop
If perchance he dropped a piece of gold.
For a marquis does not bow for money;
He only bows before God's Face,

Before the Virgin — then before noble women,
And before the king's angry brow.
He would stoop for gold were he to think:
God sees thee — thou art one of His servants.

Do not think you are too good for modest values
Which the Lord has given you for your well-being.
If picking up gold is beneath your station,
What did you seek in Eldorado's land?

Conceit

There is righteous pride, even in the wise;
A man with this pride can live in humility before God.
But righteous conceit there never was,
For arrogant pride means deviation into bitterness.

Pride is often noble — sometimes ridiculous;
Conceit as such is a diabolical thing.

Humility

Ibn 'Arabī wrote: humility is
Too precious to make a show of it;
The Sufi practices it inwardly for God —
No matter what people say in the marketplace.

El Pilar

Die Virgen del Pilar in Saragossa
Steht auf dem Pfeiler, wo Maria stand;
Andacht und Sitte kleiden sie in Seide –
Sie trägt ein golden strahlendes Gewand.

Die Heilge Jungfrau, wie mit Engelsschwingen
Kam aus der Ferne in das fremde Land,
Um Segen in die neue Welt zu bringen –
Tröstung und Gnaden von des Himmels Strand.

So kam die Heilge Jungfrau auch zu mir –
Ein Strahl von Gott durch meines Herzens Tür.
Der Himmel strahlt in unsre Welt hinein –
Mögest auch du des Wunders Pfeiler sein.

Ausruhen

Die müde Seele möchte manchmal ruhen
Und wie ein Kind nach einem Spielzeug greifen –
Nach einem Buch etwa mit schönen Bildern,
Oder im Garten, wo die Früchte reifen.

Dies ist nicht Kleinheit; es ist die Natur,
Die ihre Rechte hat; Ruh hat ihr Gutes.
Die Seele trägt den schweren Leib; der Geist
Des Frommen lebt im Kreislauf seines Blutes.

El Pilar

The *Virgen del Pilar* in Saragossa
Stands on the pillar where the Virgin stood;
Custom and devotion clothe her in silk –
She wears a dress that shines with gold.

The Holy Virgin, as on angel's wings,
Came from afar to the foreign land
To bring a blessing to a new world –
Solace and graces from Heaven's shore.

Thus came the Virgin also to me –
A ray from God to my heart's door.
Heaven sends rays into our world –
Mayest thou too be the wonderful pillar.

Resting

The weary soul sometimes wishes to rest
And, like a child, to reach for a toy –
For a book with beautiful pictures,
Or in a garden where the fruits are ripening.

This is not littleness, it is nature,
Which has its rights; repose has its good.
The soul carries the body's weight;
The spirit of the pious dwells in his very blood.

Pole

Mathematik und Eros sind zwei Pole
Die a priori auseinanderstreben,
Doch andrerseits sich mühelos verbinden –
Sonst gäb es keine Geistesruh im Leben.

Wir sind in dieser rätselhaften Welt
Wie mit verschiednen Seelen – und dabei
Bedürfen wir der beiden Pole Drang,
Auf dass der Seele Leben Eines sei.

So ist es mit den Paaren: ehelich
Sind sie vereint; doch jeder ist für sich.

Der Schatz

„Da wo dein Schatz ist, da ist auch dein Herz“ –
Man liebt das Eine aus verschiednen Gründen.
Man liebt es aus des Glaubens tiefem Trost –
Man liebt es, um des Daseins Sinn zu finden.

Des Menschen Herz birgt eine tiefe Frage:
Was ist das Dasein und was ist sein Sinn?
Gewissheit ist der weisen Seele Glück –
Der Wahrheit Licht.
„Ich bin Der, der Ich bin.“

Poles

Mathematics and Eros are two poles
Which *a priori* pull in opposite directions,
Yet on the other hand effortlessly combine –
Otherwise in life there would be no peace of mind.

We live in this world of riddles
As if with different souls – and thus
We need the impetus of both poles,
So that the soul's life may be one.

So it is with couples: in marriage
They are united; yet each stands alone.

The Treasure

"Where thy treasure is, there will thy heart be also" –
We love the One for different reasons.
We love It for the deep consolation of faith –
We love It to discover the meaning of existence.

Man's heart harbors a profound question:
What is existence and what is its meaning?
Certitude is the wise soul's happiness –
The light of Truth.
"I am That I am."

Das Heilige

Das Heilge ist das höchste Gut; doch wessen?
„Ihr sollt das Heilge nicht den Hunden geben."
Die Sache hat auch eine andre Seite:

„Ihr sollt das Heilge aus dem Dunkel heben –
Denn besser ist verschenken als vergessen."
Wahrheit ist Mitte; Wahrheit ist auch Weite.

„Man stellt ein Licht nicht unter einen Scheffel" –
So leuchte es, dass es die Seelen leite.

Problematik

Ihr habt euch mit Problemen abgeschunden –
Nur weiser Sinn kann sich zum Kreise runden.

Philosophie – eine verzwickte Schraube,
Wenn ihr so wollt. Dann besser ist der Glaube.

Tiefe

Unendlichkeit – sie ist das selge Land:
Ein Kern der Seligkeit in deiner Hand.
Leg doch der Psyche Gaukelei beiseite,
Auf dass dir nicht des Geistes Glück entgleite –

Das Jetzt, das alle Seligkeit umfasst,
Die du seit je in deiner Tiefe hast.

The Holy

The holy is the highest good; but whose?
"Ye should not give what is holy to dogs."
There is another side to this question:

"Ye should lift the holy out of darkness –
For it is better to give it away than to forget."
Truth is center; Truth is also expanse.

"One does not put a candle under a bushel" –
So let it shine, that it may guide souls.

Problematic

You have worn yourselves out with problems –
Only a wise mind can round itself into a circle.

Philosophy – a complicated screw,
If you so wish. Better than this is faith.

Depth

Infinity – it is the blissful land:
A seed of blissfulness in thine own hand.
Put aside the psyche's deceiving play,
Lest the spirit's happiness slip from thee –

The Now which all the bliss embraces
That thou hast since ever in thy depth.

Die Last

Es ist nicht so, dass nur die Bösen leiden
Und nicht die Guten. Auch die Heilgen litten
Wie andre Menschen; doch sie sind beschützt –
Begnadet, wenn sie gegen Teufel stritten.

Das Böse muss man irgendwie erschöpfen,
Und auch der Beste hilft, die Last zu tragen.
Mysterium der Natur – warum er leidet,
Darüber soll der Mensch Gott nicht befragen.

Gnaden

Die Gnade wartet, will Behälter haben –
Sie hängt am Himmel wie ein Frühlingsregen;
Schaut auf die Erde, ob sie dankbar sei –
In reine Herzen will die Gnad sich legen.

Und sie wirkt Wunder, wenn der Herr es will –
Du kannst des Höchsten Pläne nicht durchschauen.
Er offenbart sein Mitleid, seine Macht –
Will euren Seelen goldne Brücken bauen.

Geduld und Glaube

Gibt es nicht Menschen, deren Amt es ist,
Schuldlos für andrer Menschen Schuld zu büßen?
Es ist ihr Weg; ihr Mittel ist Geduld;
Mög sich viel Gnade in ihr Herz ergießen.

Geduld und Glaube; böse Wünsche fliehen.
Im Voraus ist dem Leidensheld verziehen.

The Burden

It is not true that only the bad suffer,
And not the good. Even the saints have suffered
Like other men; yet they are protected –
Covered by grace when they fight against the devil.

One must exhaust the bad one way or another,
And even the best help to bear the burden.
Mystery of nature – why does man suffer?
One should not put this question to God.

Graces

Grace is waiting, it wants to have containers –
It hangs in the sky like a spring shower;
It looks down on the earth to see if she is thankful –
Grace wishes to rest in pure hearts.

And it works wonders when the Lord so wills –
Thou canst not penetrate the plans of the Most High.
He manifests His Mercy and His Might –
He wants to build golden bridges for your souls.

Patience and Faith

Are there not men whose function it is
Guiltless to atone for other people's guilt?
It is their Path; their means is patience;
May much grace pour into their hearts.

Patience and faith: bad desires flee.
The hero of suffering is forgiven in advance.

Apostel

Und es gibt Menschen, deren Weg es ist,
Der Gotteswahrheit eine Bahn zu brechen;
„Es kam die Wahrheit und das Eitle floh" –
Lasst sie der Götzen Blendwerk niederbrechen!

Für wahres Wort, das ihr der Welt gegeben,
Gibt Gott euch neues Licht und neues Leben.

Das Zeichen

Fern ist das Ziel, wer kann es wohl erreichen?
Wenn es dir fern scheint, schaue auf das Zeichen,
Das alles ist: ob Inschrift oder Laut;
Gott hat die Brücke für dein Herz erbaut.

Des Allerhöchsten goldne Namensschrift
Sei stets vor dir. Man kann auch andres sagen:
Des Allerhöchsten Namens Laut – du sollst
Ihn stets in deinem tiefsten Innern tragen.

Constantia

Schwer ist, des Daseins Launen zu ertragen –
Wohl denen, die das Weltspiel überragen,
Gleichgültig, ob das Schicksal Gunst erweise.

„Doch ich bin standhaft wie des Nordens Stern"
Sagt Shakespeares Caesar. Also auch der Weise –
Er bleibt, was er geworden, treu dem Herrn,

In seiner Seele wechselvollen Reise
Zum Einen, wandellosen Gute hin.
Sprach doch der Herr: „Ich bin Der, der Ich bin."

Apostles

And there are men whose Path it is
To clear the way for God's Truth;
"Truth has come and vanity is fled" –
Let them break down the idols' deceit!

For the true word that you have given to the world,
God will give you new light and new life.

The Sign

Far is the goal; who can ever reach it?
When it seems far to thee, look upon the Sign
That is everything: be it inscription or sound –
God has built the bridge for thy heart.

Let the golden Name-inscription of the Most High
Be ever before thee. One could also say:
The sound of the Name of the Most High – thou shouldst
Carry it ever in thy deepest core.

Constantia

It is difficult to bear the caprices of existence –
Happy are those who soar above the world's play,
Indifferent to whether destiny shows them favor.

"But I am constant as the northern star,"
Says Shakespeare's Caesar. So too the wise man –
He remains what he has become, true to the Lord,

In his soul's changeful journey
To the one, changeless Good.
Has not the Lord said: "I am That I am."

Der Sinn

„Des Menschen Wille ist sein Himmelreich“ –
Des Menschen Himmelreich ist auch sein Wille:
Denn wenn der Mensch erkennt, dann will sein Geist,
Dass sich des tief Erkannten Sinn erfülle.

Das heißt: wenn du erkannt hast, dass der Sinn
Des Alls und deiner selbst liegt im „Ich bin“
Des Allerhöchsten, wirst du nicht mehr streben
Dich selbst abseits des Einen zu verleben.

Der Sieg

„Ich kam, und sah, und siegte“ – also sprach
Nach einem Sieg ein Held; und also spricht
Die Gotteswahrheit, die zum Herzen kommt,
Wenn sie das Tor der Finsternis zerbricht.

Denn: vincit omnia Veritas. Bewahren
Soll stets dein Herz das lichte Schwert des Wahren.

Die Winzer

„Spät kommt ihr, doch ihr kommt“ – es ist oft spät,
Doch nie zu spät, um sich zu Gott zu kehren.
Ihr kennt das Gleichnis von der letzten Stunde
Der Winzer: spätes Werk ist auch in Ehren.

Denkt nicht, dass Alterswerk an Schwäche leide,
Nichts könnt ersetzen früher Jahre Zucht;
Oft liegt im letzten Werk, dank seiner Freude,
Erneuter Glaube und erhöhte Wucht.

Gleichgültig ist, wann ihr das Gute tut;
Es heißt: Wenn Ende gut, dann alles gut.

Meaning

"Man's will is his Kingdom of Heaven" –
Man's Kingdom of Heaven is also his will:
For when man knows, his intellect wills
That the meaning deeply known may be fulfilled.

This means: if thou hast realized that the meaning
Of the All and of thyself lies in the "I am"
Of the All-Highest, thou wilt no longer seek
To squander thy life apart from the One.

Victory

"I came, I saw, I conquered" – thus spake
A hero after a victory; and thus speaks
God's Truth, that comes to the heart,
Shattering the gates of darkness.

For *vincit omnia Veritas*. Ever should
Thy heart preserve the bright sword of the True.

The Laborers in the Vineyard

"Late come ye, but yet ye come" – it is often late,
But never too late, to turn to God.
You know the parable of the eleventh hour,
Of the laborers in the vineyard: late work is also honored.

Do not think the work of old-age suffers from weakness,
That nothing can replace the discipline of early years;
In the last work, thanks to its joy, there often lies
Renewed faith and heightened strength.

It matters not when you do good;
It is said: If the end is good, then all is good.

Der Siebente

Himmelsrichtungen sind wie Leitgedanken:
Nord, Süd, Ost, West – Zenith und Nadir dann;
Die sechs Mysterien, die den Weg begleiten,
Und ohne welche keiner vorwärts kann.

Den siebten Leitgedanken möcht ich nennen:
Wenn wir den Geist in edlen Formen kennen;
Die Schönheit, die des Herzens Auge sieht –
Die nicht nach außen, die nach Innen zieht.

Die Fülle

Manchmal versteht man Menschen, doch nicht Gott;
Manchmal versteht man Gott, nicht Menschenseelen.
Man kann verstehn, dass Gott die Welt gemacht;
Nicht, dass die Menschen andre Menschen quälen.

Dir sei Genüge, dass das Gute ist –
Es gäb kein Gut, wenn Höchstes Gut nicht wäre.
An dieses halte dich, sein Horn ist voll –
Gott ist die Fülle. Und der Rest ist Leere.

Neugeburt

Aus Zufall ist gar mancher Mensch geboren;
Aus Zufall werden allzuviele sterben.
Es kann geschehen, dass sie Gott begegnen
Und so die Kron der Menschenwürde erben –

Und aus dem Zufall wird Notwendigkeit;
Wer sich mit Gott verbindet, der muss sein.
Er ist aus Gott heraus wie neugeboren –
Dem Kleinsten wird der Herr sein Nichts verzeihn.

The Seventh

The directions of space are like guiding thoughts:
North, South, East, West – then Zenith and Nadir;
The six mysteries that accompany the Path
And without which no one can advance.

The seventh guiding thought I wish to mention:
When we recognize the Spirit in noble forms;
Beauty, which the eye of the heart beholds –
Which draws us, not outward, but to the Inward.

Fullness

Sometimes one understands men, but not God;
Sometimes one understands God, but not human souls.
One can understand that God made the world,
But not that men should torment other men.

Let it suffice thee that the Good exists –
There would be no good, if the Sovereign Good were not.
Hold fast to this, its horn is full –
God is fullness. And the rest is void.

Rebirth

Many a man indeed is born by chance,
And by chance all too many will die.
But it can happen that they meet God,
And thus inherit the crown of human dignity –

And out of chance comes necessity;
Whoever binds himself to God, he has to be.
He is as if born anew out of the Most High –
The Lord will forgive the smallest one his nothingness.

Widerspruch

Die Frage stellt sich, ob es Zufall gebe;
Die Antwort ist wie manchmal: ja und nein.
Gäb's keinen Zufall, gäb's auch nicht das Wort;
Doch andrerseits, gewiss: was ist, muss sein.

Ob es uns klar ist oder ob wir streiten –
Gott wird allein unsre Geschicke leiten.

Astrologie

Die Astrologen sagen, was geschrieben,
Steht fest, trotz aller unsrer Wunschgedanken.
Es gibt ein Schicksal; deshalb auch das Wort –
Es ist nicht möglich, dass die Sterne schwanken.

Des Schicksals Form steht fest, doch dessen Weise
Ist ganz in Gottes Hand. Die Sterne zeigen,
Du sollest sterben, und du stirbst im Geiste
Und lebst noch lang – nur Seelentrug muss schweigen.

Gestirne können uns die Zukunft schildern;
Doch Gott ist frei, des Fatums Zorn zu mildern.

Prüfungen

Prüfungen müssen sein auf dieser Erde;
Wir sind aus einem Stoff gemacht, der leicht
Verdirbt, wenn nichts zur Ordnung ruft; wenn ihn
Nicht früh genug ein Wink des Herrn erreicht.

Klagt nicht, das Schicksal hab die Seel zerrissen;
Denn was uns hilft, wird Gott am besten wissen.

Contradiction

The question can be asked, whether chance exists;
The answer, as is at times the case, is: yes and no.
If chance did not exist, neither would the word;
But on the other hand, certainly: what is, must be.

Whether this is clear to us, or whether we debate –
God alone will lead our destinies.

Astrology

Astrologers say that what is written
Is predetermined, despite all our wishful thinking.
There is destiny, and therefore also the word –
It is not possible that the stars should waver.

The form of destiny is fixed, yet its mode
Is wholly in God's Hands. The stars may show
That you will die, and you die in spirit
And live yet a long time – only soul-illusion must be silent.

The stars may portray the future to us,
But God is free to ease the wrath of fate.

Trials

Trials there must be upon this earth;
We are made of a stuff that easily
Corrupts when nothing calls to order, when a sign
From the Lord does not reach us soon enough.

Do not complain that destiny has rent your soul;
For God knows best what will help us.

Aufstieg

Nur in der Mitte ist ein Weg nach Oben.
Der Mensch ist an des Daseins Rand gebunden;
Ließ ihn der Herr die goldne Mitte finden,
Dann hat sein suchend Herz den Herrn gefunden.

Gottesbewusstsein, mit ihm Gottesliebe –
Rettende Mitte in des Trugs Getriebe.
Die Anziehung, die deinen Pfad belebt,
Ist auch die Macht, die dich nach Oben hebt.

Sag nicht

Sag nicht, du seist am Ende deines Weges,
Seist schon am Ziel, nichts sei mehr zu bedauern;
Das Ziel ist endlos, doch auf Gottes Weise –
Denn das Unendliche hat keine Mauern.

Vier Heiligtümer

Vier Heiligtümer gibt es in der Welt:
Da ist der Bau mit Gottes Gegenwart;
Da ist der Wald, die Steppe, die Natur;
Da ist der Leib, mit edler Seel gepaart;

Da ist das Herz, das Gott die Treue schwur.

Ascension

Only at the Center is there a path upward.
Man is bound to the rim of existence;
If the Lord lets him find the golden Center,
Then will his searching heart have found the Lord.

God-consciousness and with it love of God —
The saving Center in the tumult of illusion.
The attraction that animates thy path
Is also the power that lifts thee heavenward.

Say Not

Say not that thou art at the end of thy path,
Already at the goal, with nothing more to regret;
The goal is endless, but in the manner of God —
For the Unending has no walls.

Four Sanctuaries

Four sanctuaries exist in the world:
There is the building with God's Presence;
There is virgin nature, forest and steppe;
There is the body, paired with a noble soul;

There is the heart, that has sworn fidelity to God.

Die Arznei

Misstrauen ist ein Gift, das Satan braut,
Uns in den engen Raum des Trugs zu bannen;
Wohl dem, der diesen Spuk in Stücke haut –
Und sieh, der Böse schwankt und flieht von dannen.

Wenn dich der Feind betrübet, schau nicht hin –
Nichtwissenwollen ist die Medizin.
Wolle nicht wissen, was die andern brüten –

Gott weiß es. Und Er wird dein Herz behüten,
Der Dinge Wesen ist in seinen Händen.

Die Wahrheit siegt; damit lass es bewenden.

Zweiseitigkeit

Schwere und Leichtigkeit sind doppelsinnig:
Das Erste zieht nach unten, hält gefangen;
Der zweite Trieb zerstreut nach allen Seiten;

Doch ist das Schwere auch der Erd Verlangen
Zu festigen und Gleichgewicht zu geben;
Die Leichtigkeit hebt uns zu Himmels Weiten.

So mög das Herz zur heilgen Tiefe streben
Und ebenso zur heilgen Höh gelangen;
Mögen Zenith und Nadir uns begleiten!

Remedy

Suspicion is a poison brewed by Satan
In order to imprison us in the narrow space of deceit.
Happy the one who shatters this specter –
And see, the evil one falters and flees away.

Whenever the Enemy troubles thee, pay no heed –
Not-wanting-to-know is the remedy.
Do not seek to know what others are scheming –

God knows it. And He will protect thy heart,
The nature of all things lies in His Hands.

Truth will be victorious; leave it at that.

Ambiguity

Heaviness and lightness are equivocal in meaning:
The first pulls downward, keeps imprisoned;
The second force scatters in all directions.

But the heavy is also earth's desire
To give stability and equilibrium;
Lightness lifts us up to Heaven's expanse.

So may the heart strive toward holy depth
And likewise attain holy height;
May zenith and nadir accompany us!

Der Gläubige

Da war ein Heiligtum mit Schriftgelehrten,
Welche den Eingang einem Mann verwehrten,
Der nichts von ihrer Wissenschaft verstand;
So blieb er an des heilgen Ortes Rand.

Auch das war der gelehrten Schar zuviel;
So ging er weg und irrte ohne Ziel,
Und hielt ein winzig Steinchen in der Hand,
Das in der Näh des Heiligtums er fand –

Und wanderte bis an des Meeres Strand.
Und dort entschlief er. Und der kleine Stein
Bracht ihn zum Himmel, sich an Gott zu freun.

Liebesfreiheit

„Liebe den Herrn und tue, was du willst" –
So sprach ein Heiliger. Die Gottesminne
Verbrennt das Böse: Hochmut, Bitterkeit;
Der wahrhaft Fromme ist sich dessen inne.

Und hättest du höchsten Verdienst erworben –
Ein Tropfen Bitternis hätt es verdorben.
In Demut, Milde und Erhabenheit,
Zur höchsten Gnade ist dein Herz bereit.

The Believer

There was a sanctuary with scholars of scripture,
Who refused entrance to a man
Because he understood nothing of their science;
So he stood on the boundary of the sacred place.

Even this was too much for that learned group,
So he went his way and wandered without aim,
And in his hand he held a tiny stone
Which near the sanctuary he had found –

He wandered till he reached the ocean's shore,
And there he died. The little stone
Brought him to Heaven, in God to take delight.

Love's Freedom

"Love the Lord and do what thou wilt" –
Thus spoke a saint. The love of God
Burns up evil: pride, bitterness;
The truly pious man is conscious of this.

Even hadst thou earned the highest merit –
A drop of bitterness would spoil it all.
In humility, gentleness and serenity,
Thy heart is ready for the highest Grace.

Alhambra

„Nicht gibt es einen Sieger außer Gott" –
Dies steht an der Alhambra Wand geschrieben.
„Das Wahre kam, das Eitle ist verweht" –
So soll der Erde Trug dich nicht betrüben.

Es liegt ein Sinn in jeglichem Geschick;
Zukunft ist Gott – das Gute kommt zurück.
Dies meint der Spruch an der Alhambra Wände –
Anfang und Ende reichen sich die Hände.

Undank

Wenn ihr in einer guten Lage seid,
Dann betet nicht, Gott mög sie besser machen;
Dankt Gott dafür, dass gut die Lage ist;
Sonst könntet ihr des Höchsten Zorn entfachen.

Seid dankbar für das Gute, das ihr heute
Besitzt; auf dass euch nicht das Gut entgleite.
Seht zu: ihr habt schon viel, ihr wollt noch mehr;
Des Undankbaren Hände werden leer.

Alhambra

"There is no victor if it be not God" –
This is written on the Alhambra's walls.
"The True has come, and vanity is fled" –
So earth's illusion should not trouble thee.

There lies a meaning in each destiny;
The future is God – the Good returns.
The verse on the Alhambra's walls means this –
Beginning and end clasp each other's hand.

Ingratitude

If you are in a good situation,
Then do not pray that God make it better;
Thank God that the situation is good,
Otherwise you might kindle His Wrath.

Be thankful for the good that you possess
Today, so that it may not slip away from you.
See: you already have much, you want still more;
The hands of the ungrateful will be empty.

Spott

„Wohl dem, der nicht sitzt, wo die Spötter sitzen" –
Gott straft die Satansbrut mit ihren Witzen.
Ob ihnen Trug auch halbe Siege brächte –
An seinem eignen Gift erstickt der Schlechte.

Und es ist klar: es spottet der Gerechte
Des Spötters, so wie Gott den Trug verlacht –
Des Spötters, der sein Seelenheil verzechte
Um des Vergnügens einer kurzen Nacht.

Des Frommen Spott ist Antwort; doch an sich
Berührt ihn nicht, was der Verleumder macht –
Ein eitler Spuk, der in das Nichts entwich.

Psalmwort

Der König hatte Lust an dem Gesetz:
„Und redet vom Gesetze Tag und Nacht."
Und der Gerechte – sprach er – „wist ein Baum
Der, wenn es Zeit, hat gute Frucht gebracht."

Den Baum der Seele sollst du treulich hegen –
Und sollst die Frucht vor Gottes Füße legen.

Tröstung

Gott schickt uns Tröste, die uns klein erscheinen –
Zu Unrecht, denn sogar im kleinsten Troste
Liegt Gottes Güte, und ein tiefer Sinn,
Die überwiegen, was das Herz erboste –
Und löschen, was das wunde Herz betrübte;
Belebend, was die Seel im Stillen liebte.

Das fernste Gut mag schimmern auch im nächsten –
Im Kleinsten ist ein Hinweis auf den Höchsten.

Scoffing

"Blessèd is he who sitteth not with the scornful" –
God punishes the devil's brood with their bad jokes.
Even if their deceit should bring them partial victories –
The wicked one will choke on his own venom.

And it is obvious: the just man scoffs at the scoffer,
Just as God laughs at the illusion –
Of the scoffer, who has forfeited his soul's salvation
For the pleasures of a passing night.

The scorn of the pious man is a rejoinder;
But in himself he is not touched by the slanderer's deed –
An empty specter that vanishes into nothingness.

A Verse from the Psalms

The king took pleasure in the Law:
"And he talked about the Law day and night."
The just man – he said – "is a tree
Which, in due course, bears good fruit."

Thou shalt faithfully tend the tree of the soul –
And thou shalt lay its fruit at God's feet.

Consolation

God sends us consolations that seem small to us –
But wrongly so, for even in the smallest consolation
Lie God's Goodness and a profound meaning,
Which outweigh what angered our heart –
And erase what saddened our wounded heart,
Quickening what the soul loves in stillness.

The furthest good may also shimmer through the nearest –
In the smallest thing is a pointer to the Highest.

Urwissen

Fragt nicht, was euch geschehe nach dem Tod.
Fragt nicht, da ihr es wisst im tiefsten Innern:
Ihr seid unsterblich. Und dass Seligkeit
Das Sein ist – euer Herz kann sich erinnern.

Weil ihr tief in die Sinnenwelt verstrickt,
Habt ihr die tiefre Wirklichkeit vergessen.
Sagt nicht, der Irrtum sei nicht eure Schuld –
Gott wird die Kräfte eurer Seele messen.

Auferstehung

Alles, was ist – so heißt es – lobt den Herrn.
Schon unser bloßes Dasein ist gewaltig,
Ein wahres Wunder; so der Dinge Werte
Und Mächte. Und die Welt ist vielgestaltig

Weil Gott unendlich ist. Ihr habt die Wahl
Zwischen dem Nichts und Gott. Und dieses sehen,
Ist mehr als Denken; es ist lichtes Sein
In eurem Herzen – es ist Auferstehen.

Primordial Knowledge

Do not ask what befalls you after death.
Do not ask, because you know it in your deepest core:
You are immortal. And that bliss
Is Being — your heart can remember.

Because you are tangled deep in the world of senses,
You have forgotten the deeper reality.
Do not say the error is not your fault —
God will measure the strengths of your soul.

Resurrection

It is written: all that is, praiseth the Lord.
Indeed, our mere existence is prodigious,
A true miracle; so too are the qualities
And powers of things. The world is multiform

Because God is infinite. Ye have the choice
Between nothingness and God. And to see this
Is more than thinking; it is luminous Being
Within your heart — yea, it is Resurrection.

Index of Foreign Quotations

(Page numbers refer to the quotations as they occur in the English translations)

A Note on the Translations

The author considered his poems didactic in nature and termed them *Sinngedichte* (meaning-poems) or *Lehrgedichte* (teaching-poems). In one sense, these poems lend themselves to translation because the accent is on their meaning, which is in no way diminished by being expressed in a new language. Yet in another sense, poetic and musical values are so closely intertwined with the genius of the original language that they cannot be adequately reproduced in translation, and here much in the domain of onomatopoeia, as well as rhythm and melody, must be lost. Added to this is the fact that the sound of German possesses a certain majesty and force, in which one senses the raw power of nature—towering mountains, deep lakes, mysterious forests—which the gentler tones of English, and its milder landscape of sound, are not able to convey. Thus a bilingual edition is of great value, for it allows the reader who has only a modest knowledge of German to appreciate the original poetry in all its resonance. Schuon himself was more concerned with maintaining the integrity of the content than with trying to reproduce the poetic and musical qualities of the style, and he always preferred a more direct or literal translation. To this end, every attempt has been made to provide a literal rendering of the German text that remains as true as possible to the author's meaning, and at the same time to do so in a form that, without pretending to be poetry, nonetheless possesses a dignity and grace befitting its subject. These translations are the work of William Stoddart, Catherine Schuon and Tamara Pollack.

* * *

"Each language is a soul," Schuon has written, paraphrasing Aristotle; that is to say, a "psychic or mental dimension." A language is thus a mode of thought, imagination, and feeling, as well as of expression. Even the simple goal of a literal translation proves difficult in practice, for there are rarely exact equivalences between languages, and many images and nuances cannot be conveyed. At times German is more synthetic than English; for example, the German word "*Geist*," which appears frequently in these poems, can mean alternately "mind," "spirit," or "intellect"— terms which in a metaphysical context describe significant differences of meaning, and the translator must judge from the context which meaning is most appropriate. At other times, a distinction exists in German but not in English. For example, the word *Erkenntnis*—which can mean knowledge, recognition, or realization—is distinguished from a more factual and quantitative type of knowledge conveyed by *Wissen*. Although *Erkenntnis* also has more ordinary meanings, its deepest sense converges on gnosis; and although *Wissen* can also describe true metaphysical discernment, it often connotes simply an expertise, erudition, or mastery of a body of information (in fact the German for "science" is *Wissenschaft*). In these poems *Erkenntnis* generally refers to intellectual intuition, visionary knowledge that is a "seeing" rather than a mere "thinking," as for example in the poems "*Erkennen*" ("True Knowledge") and "*Skepsis*" ("Skepticism"). We have translated it as knowledge or discernment according to the context, and sometimes as "true knowledge," or with a capital letter, to indicate that it belongs to the spiritual order.

It may also happen that there is a perfect fusion between language and meaning in the German text, in a way which has no counterpart in English. For example, the poem "In Other Words" begins "*Ursein, Sein, Dasein*": "Beyond-Being, Being, and Existence." But *Dasein* is literally —or etymologically—"There-Being," so that in German all three words are built on the foundation of *Sein*: "Being" is framed on one side by that which transcends it (*Ur-*), and on the other by that which particularizes or conditions it (*Da-*). The poet's metaphysical wisdom is embedded in the language itself, and this appears yet again in the definition that immediately follows: Beyond-Being is "*unpersönlich*" (non-personal), Being is "*persönlich*" (personal), and Existence is "*vielpersönlich*" (multi-personal). Here again words, in their very structure, conform to the metaphysical hierarchy they enunciate.

In yet other instances the "flavor" or valence of a word is different, even when the meaning is more or less the same. This is especially true of down-to-earth, homely words that have become informal or slang in English, but are still proper in German. For example, the word "*Kram*," which the author often uses to refer to the unimportance and triviality of earthly "stuff," as in the phrase "*eitler Erdenkram*" ("vain earthly triviality" or "rubbish"), is most literally translated as "junk." But the English "junk" is simply too colloquial to fit the context. Words like "triviality," "dross," or "vanity," on the other hand, are too elevated to convey the way "*Erdenkram*" instantly deflates the false importance we attach to worldly things. In this case, there is simply no good equivalent in English, and we have had to settle for compromises.

There is also the question of the effect of words. The German language, as the author has oftentimes remarked, is symbolic and imaginatively rich. German words paint pictures in the mind, making it a particularly powerful language for poetry. For example, in the poem "Archetypal Man" the line "*Sieh, wie der Dinge Rätsel sich verzweigen—*" ("See how the enigma of things ramifies—") evokes the image of the riddle or mystery of things branching out in different directions, like the diverging limbs of a tree; "*Zweig*" means literally the branch of a tree. In German, the word is simultaneously a picture and a concept, the concept being expressed by means of a picture; the English "ramifies" contains the same meaning etymologically (from the Latin *ramus* or branch), but in English it functions purely as an abstract concept.

In German this picture can be embedded in the structure of the words themselves, which are often compounds, attaching one word to another. On one occasion the author calls our attention to this very fact: the word "*Sinnbild*," composed of "*Sinn*" (mind, meaning, significance) and "*Bild*" (image or picture), means etymologically a mental image or a "meaning-picture," thus, most commonly, a "symbol." In the poem "Figurative Art," the author hyphenates the word ("*Sinn-Bilder*") to remind us of its component parts: it is simultaneously "symbols" and "meaning-pictures." Nuances such as these can rarely be preserved in translation, and here we have simply rendered "*Sinn-Bilder*" as "symbols."

German affords a great deal of freedom in the coining of new words by combining two or more existing words together. English allows this kind of freedom to a certain extent, and more so in poetry than prose, though by hyphenating words rather than compounding them. We have taken advantage of this "poetic license" in several instances, with an eye to giving the reader a flavor of these "meaning-pictures" painted by the German words. For example, in the poem "*Realitas*" the author coins the word "*An-sich-sein*" to describe the ipseity of the Supreme Being. We have rendered this neologism as "In-itself-hood," which better conveys the immediacy of meaning of "*An-sich-sein*" than the more abstract, philosophical term "ipseity," though they mean effectively the same thing. Sometimes, however, this approach has not been possible. Thus in the poem "Continuation," the line "*Das Festgeronnene, das Fortbewegte,*" referring respectively to form and number, defies literal translation. "Crystallization and movement," as we have translated it, conveys the concept though not the "picture." The "picture" juxtaposes something which has been "congealed" or "made solid" with something that has been "moved away," "propelled" or "set into forward motion"—a literal translation of this line might be "The firm-solidified and the moved-along." With just two words the poem evokes the change of state from fluidity into something fixed (the static nature of form), and the setting into motion away from a central point (the dynamism of number).

The author's punctuation is bold and vigorous, and part of his poetic style. Oftentimes he will use a long dash or full colon in place of a complete sentence; the effect is to focus the attention on the essential words, often nouns, allowing the connecting words to remain implicit.[1] This creates a highly concentrated, essentialized language that takes us right to the heart of things. In English we have tried to keep the majority of these constructions, recognizing that this is an important element of the author's style, for form is not simply a question of individual preference; it reflects and is informed by content. In some instances, however, the effect of this punctuation sounds awkward and disjointed in English, and tends to obscure rather than contribute to the meaning. In German the rhythm of the verse and the harmony of rhyme provide an element of gentleness and musicality which compensate the rigor of the diction. Lacking this balancing element in English, we have thought it better occasionally to soften the punctuation and add some of the connecting words.

* * *

We hope, with these few examples, to have offered a glimpse of the vividness and richness with which these poems resonate in the original. The author has called poetry "melodious thought," for it blends metaphysics with music and awakens the vision of the heart:

Dialektik überzeugt uns mit Ideen,
Sodass die Dinge wir abstrakt verstehen;
Die Dichtung hat Gefühl, sie wirkt mit Bildern
Und will, dadurch, des Denkens Strenge mildern —
Dass wir das Wahre mit dem Herzen sehen.

Dialectic convinces us with ideas,
So that we may understand things abstractly;
Poetry has feeling, it works with images
And seeks thereby to soften the austerity of thought —
So that we may see the True with our heart.

(*World Wheel*, Second Collection, II)

—Tamara Pollack

[1] A "*Gedankenstrich*" (a long dash) means literally a "thought-dash," and functions as a pause for reflection before the completion or conclusion of a thought.

Index of Titles
German and English

BOOKS BY FRITHJOF SCHUON

The Transcendent Unity of Religions (1953, 1984)
Spiritual Perspectives and Human Facts (1954, 1970, 1987, 2007)
Gnosis: Divine Wisdom (1959, 1978, 1990, 2006)
Language of the Self (1959, 1999)
Castes and Races (1959, 1982)
Stations of Wisdom (1961, 1980, 1995)
Understanding Islam (1963, 1972, 1986, 1998)
Light on the Ancient Worlds (1965, 1984, 2006)
Treasures of Buddhism (In the Tracks of Buddhism) (1968, 1989, 1993)
Logic and Transcendence (1975, 1984, 2009)
Esoterism as Principle and as Way (1981, 1990)
Sufism: Veil and Quintessence (1981, 2006)
From the Divine to the Human (1982)
Christianity/Islam: Perspectives on Esoteric Ecumenism (1985, 2008)
Survey of Metaphysics and Esoterism (1986, 2000)
In the Face of the Absolute (1989, 1994)
The Feathered Sun: Plains Indians in Art and Philosophy (1990)
To Have a Center (1990)
Roots of the Human Condition (1991, 2002)
Images of Primordial and Mystic Beauty: Paintings by Frithjof Schuon (1992)
Echoes of Perennial Wisdom (1992)
The Play of Masks (1992)
Road to the Heart: Poems (1995)
The Transfiguration of Man (1995)
The Eye of the Heart (1997)
Form and Substance in the Religions (2002)
Adastra & Stella Maris: Poems by Frithjof Schuon (bilingual edition) (2003)
Songs without Names, Volumes I-VI: Poems by Frithjof Schuon (2006)
Songs without Names, Volumes VII-XII: Poems by Frithjof Schuon (2006)
World Wheel, Volumes I-III: Poems by Frithjof Schuon (2006)
World Wheel, Volumes IV-VII: Poems by Frithjof Schuon (2006)
Primordial Meditation: Contemplating the Real (2007)
Autumn Leaves & The Ring: Poems by Frithjof Schuon (bilingual edition) (2010)

ANTHOLOGIES OF FRITHJOF SCHUON'S WRITINGS

The Essential Frithjof Schuon, ed. Seyyed Hossein Nasr (1986, 2005)
Songs for a Spiritual Traveler: Selected Poems (bilingual edition) (2002)
René Guénon: Some Observations, ed. William Stoddart (2004)
The Fullness of God: Frithjof Schuon on Christianity, ed. James S. Cutsinger (2004)
Prayer Fashions Man: Frithjof Schuon on the Spiritual Life, ed. James S. Cutsinger (2005)
Art from the Sacred to the Profane: East and West, ed. Catherine Schuon (2007)
Splendor of the True: A Frithjof Schuon Reader, ed. James S. Cutsinger (forthcoming)